When Did
Jesus Become
Republican?

When Did Jesus Become Republican?

Rescuing Our Country and
Our Values from the Right

Stategies for a Post-Bush America

Mark Ellingsen

ROWMAN & LITTLEFIELD PUBLISHERS, INC.
Lanham • Boulder • New York • Toronto • Plymouth, UK

ROWMAN & LITTLEFIELD PUBLISHERS, INC.

Published in the United States of America
by Rowman & Littlefield Publishers, Inc.
A wholly owned subsidiary of The Rowman & Littlefield Publishing Group, Inc.
4501 Forbes Boulevard, Suite 200, Lanham, Maryland 20706
www.rowmanlittlefield.com

Estover Road
Plymouth PL6 7PY
United Kingdom

British Library Cataloguing in Publication Information Available

Library of Congress Cataloging-in-Publication Data

Ellingsen, Mark, 1949–
    When did Jesus become Republican? : rescuing our country and our values
from the right. Strategies for a post-Bush America / Mark Ellingsen.
        p. cm.
    ISBN-13: 978-0-7425-5224-1 (cloth : alk. paper)
    ISBN-10: 0-7425-5224-1 (cloth : alk. paper)
    1. Religious right—United States. 2. Christianity and politics—United States.
I. Title.
BR516.E44 2007
261.70973—dc22   2007010923

♾™ The paper used in this publication meets the minimum requirements of
American National Standard for Information Sciences—Permanence of Paper for
Printed Library Materials, ANSI/NISO Z39.48-1992.

For our newest daughter

LEAH FERGUSON ELLINGSEN

(and for Carol and Pat, the great folks who raised her)

Contents

Part III: It Will Take a Conservative Theology and a New Liberal Coalition to Recover a Politically Liberal Jesus

Acknowledgments

Being a religious adherent and a liberal Democrat always seemed logical to me, even if the majority of churchgoers these days don't see it that way. I guess it's had to do with knowing all the people I have known over the years who had no trouble relating Christianity and liberal politics. It began with that Norwegian immigrant family of mine and all the wonderful political arguments at the dinner table. Though I had only recently turned eleven in 1960, I can still remember my mother, cheered on silently by my father, arguing with our German-American pastor the Sunday before the election after he had preached a sermon urging the congregation to vote Republican against that Catholic Kennedy on account of what he might do to our constitutional system. How often I heard members of the family wonder how "the [establishment] Americans" could do minorities and the poor so dirty, when "they [those getting the shaft] were a lot more American than we were." Then I married into a largely Democratic family. (The family's few Republicans were from New England and New York, so they were still pretty liberal.) Over the years, Betsey and I have frequently engaged in conversations that arrived at a lot of the same conclusions I used to come to with my beloved parents and my extended family—wondering how someone could follow Jesus and still blame the poor for their problems.

I've associated professionally with a lot of wonderful colleagues who held together a conservative religious faith and liberal politics. So many of my colleagues and students at the Black Church's largest seminary, the Interdenominational Theological Center in Atlanta, where I am privileged to teach, embody the integration of these values, just as the African-American Church as a whole does it so well. Andrew Young and Joseph Lowery frequently show up on our campus (even on some occasions in my own classroom), modeling the integration of these commitments so well. Of course, among some of the Brothers and Sisters of our faculty and student body you can still find a handful of old-style Republicans (loyal to the Party of Lincoln), sort of like there are a couple in my extended family whom I love. That's been the beauty of how I've mixed religion and politics. There's been plenty of dialogue with Republicans, in the spirit of friendship. When you learn politics that way, then you don't let politics divide your family, your church, or your nation. That's the spirit in which I hope readers will take this book. Religious folks who don't agree with me might be just as faithful as, even more so than, I am. We just don't agree on politics.[1] This book is merely my attempt to understand why what seems so logical to me (the connection between faith and liberal politics) doesn't make sense to most Americans, and then to offer a little advice to folks who agree with me politically on what we might do to get the American public to see things our way (to help the Democratic political consultants get a few more of our people elected).

As usual, the Democrat with whom I live, Betsey, had the most formative influence on the book, through conversation and editing, and so I'm pleased to offer a special word of thanks here. Another who deserves such a thank you is Rev. Dr. W. Arthur Lewis, a colleague at my seminary and a Democratic political operative himself from his days in New Jersey state government, for keeping me from inadvertent distortions in my discussions of African-American Democratic political dispositions.

The book is dedicated to another beloved family member. It's only fair. After all, Betsey's and my other three children have each had a book dedicated to them. And so this book is dedicated to the newest member of our family, Leah. Of course, we can't take credit for raising her. Pat and Carol Ferguson, a couple of great folks, who—thanks to the wise discernment of our son Pat in marrying their daughter—are family now too, get the credit for nurturing this wonderful young lady. But we like to say she's ours as well. After all, Jesus and Democrats believe in sharing good things.

Introduction: Are All True Believers Really Conservative?

Jesus and His Gospel teach conservative values. George Bush and his Republican allies are truly men and women of God. The familiar poll data suggest that most Americans agree—especially religiously oriented citizens. Nothing in the 2006 Congressional election results suggests that these perceptions have changed or that America and its religiously oriented voters have become more liberal. Exit polls conducted by the Fourth National Survey of Religion and Politics after the 2004 elections indicated that Protestants supported Bush by a margin of 59 percent to 40 percent. Among those who worship weekly or more frequently, the margins were 58 percent to 41 percent and 64 percent to 35 percent respectively. The more you worship God, the more likely you are to vote conservative and Republican. According to 2006 exit polls conducted under the auspices of the National Election Pool for all the major networks, at least 57 percent of regular worshippers still voted for Republican Congressional candidates.

Nothing much has changed with regard to the Bush margin of victory among theologically conservative Evangelical voters. Just as his margin of victory increased in 2004 (winning 78 percent of this group compared to 72 percent in 2000), Republican candidates still won 72 percent of that constituency (approximately 24 percent of the popular vote) in 2006. A strong Biblical orientation seems to a great extent to bend you toward the conservative side (at least if you are white). Not just among white Protestants did Bush enjoy important advantages. He won the Catholic vote by 52 percent to 47 percent. Granted, Democrats won the Catholic vote in 2006, by a margin of 55 percent to 44 percent, but barely gained a majority among white Catholics and lost among those

1

attending Mass weekly (52 percent to 47 percent). Among white Protestants, the margin of victory in 2004 was of landslide proportions (67 percent to 32 percent). According to National Election Pool exit polls it was still a 61 percent to 37 percent victory for Republicans in 2006 among that constituency.

Charles Krauthammer of *The Washington Post* seems to be on target in noting that the 2006 election results are just a mild swing, not a major realignment of recent voting trends. Besides, the very close margins of victory in races in both Houses and the conservative character of the new Democratic Representatives must be noted. Most are "Clinton Democrats," and a little of the Right of him. Above all, then, according to exit poll data, the Democratic victories were achieved as a result of diminishing support for the war in Iraq, the loss of support for the Republican Congress in the wake of revelations of corruption, and increased decline of the President's approval rating.[1] The new Democratic majority is quite likely to wither as soon as these issues are removed from the media's and the public's radar screens, which at least the last three certainly will by 2008. These intuitions that the nation and its religiously inclined electorate have by no means swung to the Left seem undergirded by the fact that in the November elections, seven out of eight anti-gay amendments to state constitutions regarding marriage were passed.

It is clear that the 2006 elections have not changed the trends that equate conservative voting with religious conviction. Most Americans, especially whites who worship regularly, are involved in their church, have a politically conservative orientation, and vote Republican. It was certainly not this way in the days of the Civil Rights Movement, the Vietnam-era protests, or even in the early twentieth-century labor movements. Proponents of liberal alternatives in these cases freely and convincingly invoked Jesus and the Christian faith as allies. The Social Gospel of the early labor union movement and Martin Luther King both appealed to the Christian Gospel for authorization—in King's case even for the U.S. withdrawal from Vietnam.[2] The public, it seems, bought it. Catholic, Russian Orthodox, and many Lutheran constituencies voted Democrat. Why not today? What happened? This is a book about answering these questions, by getting to the root causes, not just the symptoms of present political dynamics, along with some concrete and practical suggestions, not just platitudes, concerning what to do about the new circumstances.

HOW WE GOT TO WHERE WE ARE:
A BRIEF OVERVIEW

It is not just Republicans and their allies on the Religious Right who have convinced America that Christianity supports conservative values, even the dismantling of the Great Society legacies. They have also gotten a lot of help from post-Clinton Democrats.

At least at the national level, Democratic candidates in 2004 stayed far away as much as possible from religious rhetoric or the "values" question so well played by Bush and friends. If Democrats did respond, they did so only by talking about faith influencing their values in a generic sense. They did not use religious language in defense of traditional Democratic convictions about justice, Affirmative Action, economic equality, or ecology. Few of the Democratic Congressional winners in 2006 who talked values went beyond advocating pro-life, antiabortion positions. Except for a handful of their pundits, it seems that Democrats are continuing to allow conservative Republicans to define the topics on which religious values have relevance (such as abortion, gay rights, and a sort of free-market understanding of freedom).

Of course to some extent, Democratic strategies in 2004 were no different than those they have employed since the ebbing of their hegemony in the 1970s. Part of it has to do with the changing character of American society. And a related factor in these changes in political loyalties among American Christians has to do with corresponding developments in America's mainline Protestant churches, as well as in American Catholicism.

In later chapters we will examine the cultural and institutional denominational factors that have worked to the advantage of the Republicans. But a more fundamental factor in these developments relates to the way in which Americans have intuitively understood religious life since the Revolution. They have done so in the categories of Puritanism, altered by developments in the nineteenth and twentieth centuries. The result has been a vision of religion conducive to the Republican agenda of small government, the promotion of free-market global economics, and furthering the interests of individualism and big business, along with conservative moral values. Since these dynamics are the framework for all the other religious, cultural, and social developments we will note, let's begin first with trying to understand this characteristically American way of looking at religion and morality.

Essentially my argument is that by presenting a conservative Jesus and a Gospel that supports the Republican agenda, Bush, his cohorts, and their post-Reagan predecessors have been able to convince the large segments of the American middle class to vote against their own economic interests. They have also been successful in silencing or distorting the prophetic social voice of historic Christianity.

In many respects my thinking about these points is in line with the recent best sellers of Jim Wallis (*God's Politics*), Bill Press (*How the Republicans Stole Christmas*), Tom Frank (*What's the Matter with Kansas?*), Michael Lerner (*The Left Hand of God*), Randall Balmer (*Thy Kingdom Come*), Bob Edgar (*Middle Church*), John Danforth (*Faith and Politics*), Barack Obama (*The Audacity of Hope*), Jimmy Carter (*Our Endangered Values*), as well as the recent book by Kathleen Kennedy Townsend (*Failing America's Faithful*). But what I have to offer here is the complete and accurate explanation of how and why the Republicans have succeeded in reinterpreting Christianity and selling it successfully to religiously inclined Americans. And although Wallis, Edgar, Balmer, Kennedy Townsend, and Press are to be commended for highlighting the New Testament Jesus Who cares more about the poor than the market, and more about justice than family values (Matthew 19:21; 8:21–22; 10:34–39; Mark 10:21), the concrete proposals of the first four of these authors, as well as to some extent Lerner's call from a Jewish perspective for a new "progressive spiritual consciousness and politics," inadvertently create some of the problems with Christian engagement in politics that the Religious Right has.[3] All of these books fail to appreciate the complexities that need to be involved if a coalition is to be built between progressive Evangelicals, black Christians, mainline white Protestants, and liberal Catholics in such a way that the Secular and Jewish Left are not marginalized in such a coalition. That is why we need this book.

Along with Bill Press, and to some extent John Danforth, Barack Obama, and Jimmy Carter, I've got another way to get to a vision for America, one more sensitive to the First Amendment and the historic Christian tradition. But even these esteemed political leaders do not have the whole story.[4] We'll get to that in the final chapters. If we don't get all the facts right on these issues, the Republican version of Christianity will continue to exert influence over our nation and the Church, no matter how much Democrats and theological liberals try to talk values and religion.

Let's summarize where we are going in the first section, trying to understand precisely how Jesus and His Gospel became conservative and Republican, why many of America's faithful have arrived at the conclusion that Republicans best embody Christian values. It starts with the profound impact that Puritanism has had on the American social psyche. In the next chapter we'll talk about that in detail. Americans intuitively think about religion in these categories and, often unconsciously, see the basic beliefs and practices of Puritanism as what defines authentic American religion.

In this regard, while affirming much of the thoughtful analysis of Kevin Phillips (*American Theocracy*), I must break with him in his argument that the dominant form of American religion which today undergirds and supports the Republican coalition has been a radicalized sectarianism.[5] Another recent book that exhibits similar problems was released last year by Chris Hedges (*American Fascists*).[6] Both Phillips and Hedges overlook how mainstream the majority of religious adherents in America have been, how only those belonging to "proper" (Puritan-related) mainline churches (Presbyterians, Episcopalians, Congregationalists, Methodists, and Baptists) have gained power and influence, and how even the "fringe" religious groups on which these authors concentrate (Pentecostals, Southern Baptists, Christian Reconstructionists, and even to some extent Mormons) have historic and theological ties to Puritanism. Phillips's thesis that mainline Protestantism was in decline as early as the 1930s overlooks this data and the hard fact that the vast majority of American Christians still belong to a coalition of these churches, historic African-American churches, or Catholicism. In fact, this coalition outnumbers Evangelicals (membership of bodies associated with the Religious Right) by almost three to one according to the most recent (2004 and 2005) membership statistics (102 million to 40 million). Another assessment, a Baylor University Religion Survey based on 2005 Gallup poll data, estimated that the mainline church–Black Church–Catholic coalition outnumbers Evangelicalism by 48 percent to 33.5 percent of the population. That the media and the political consultants keep ignoring these numbers and the importance of the members of this coalition bespeaks the dominance of the Puritan

Paradigm (the Black Church and Catholicism are not properly part of the Paradigm). It also reflects their elite biases against the mainline Protestant denominations, in part because the bourgeoisie philosophical and moral assumptions adopted by the leadership of many in these religious bodies, at least since World War II, are no longer news, and are perceived as an old-fashioned, late 1950s–early 1960s liberalism that no longer has much political clout.

As the book proceeds, we will begin to unwrap what is entailed for American attitudes by the dominance of the Puritan Paradigm on our social psyche. We will see how Puritanism stands for a largely traditional code of morality, strictly enforced. In general, it is also committed to a very conservative view of Biblical authority. Although Puritanism in its origins concerned itself with social issues, on establishing Christian commitments in the structures of society (a theocratic orientation), the enormous impact of Revivalism in America in the later decades of the nineteenth century has tended to focus its adherents and inheritors of its legacy on the individual believer and his or her salvation and personal morality, though never in such a way as totally to renounce Puritan theocratic tendencies. These convictions are embedded in the guts of many religiously inclined Americans. At various times in the twentieth century the mainline churches have failed to appeal to this set of beliefs, usually to the detriment of these denominations. Fundamentalism's political successes at the beginning of that century (a number of states followed its agenda in forbidding the teaching of Evolution in the schools) were largely a function of its ability to tap into the fundamental belief system of the transformed American version of Puritanism.

Of course Fundamentalism fell out of favor after the famous Scopes Trial over Evolution. But it was reborn again after World War II as the Evangelical Movement by a group of young Fundamentalists determined to package the old version of the faith in new ways. Led by Billy Graham, Harold Ockenga, and Carl Henry, this Movement became politically chic in 1979 with the formation of the Moral Majority by Fundamentalist Jerry Falwell, a Movement that successfully brought together the political agendas of both Fundamentalists and Evangelicals in such a way as to make a significant contribution to the election of Ronald Reagan. This coalition of Fundamentalists and Conservative Evangelicals is the core constituency of the Religious Right. Three years earlier, the media had already rediscovered this significant segment of the faithful with the Presidency of Jimmy Carter and poll results that suggested how important being "born again" was to a significant segment of the American public. As the spiritual daughter of Fundamentalism, the Evangelical Movement also tapped into the core Puritan suppositions that most Americans have imbibed. The key, then, to Republican electoral success post-Reagan has been to link up with the suppositions of Puritanism, for then religiously inclined Americans, at least subconsciously, are likely to perceive political policies and politicians who embody these convictions as both authentically American and authentically religious.

Meanwhile, the impact of German Enlightenment thought on the masses after World War II, as more and more Americans went to college and learned such worldviews, has further contributed to Republican hegemony and the perception that you have to be conservative in order to be authentically religious. The relativism associated with this school of thought—its critical mind-set toward any claims of absolute truth, along with the Sexual Revolution and the accompanying greater acceptance of homosexuality, as well as the divorce epidemic and the Feminist Movement—ran counter to the core beliefs of Puritanism and was all perceived by "Puritanized" Americans as un-Christian. In that sense, some analysts speak of the evolution of a "post-Puritan" ethos in America.[6]

These dynamics, however, led many religiously inclined Americans at the grassroots (where most Christians live) to yearn for countermovements to these dominant social trends, which were increasingly being marketed by the media and other businesses. The fact that mainline churches like Roman Catholicism, large segments of Lutheranism, and mainline denominations rooted in or aligned with Puritanism (like Presbyterianism, the United Church of Christ, Methodism, The Episcopal Church, and even for awhile the Southern Baptist Convention), leaned toward endorsing core suppositions of the German Enlightenment in order to be "relevant" further stimulated the yearning of the grassroots for an alternative. Even their own churches have left them, it sometimes seems. But the old Puritan piety was/is still alive and well at the grassroots among ordinary churchgoing Americans. Little wonder, then, that a conservative party like the post-Reagan Republicans, who seemed to reject these "disturbing" Enlightenment trends along with the "big government" Democratic bureaucracies, has successfully convinced many Americans to appropriate its version of libertarianism. The Republican agenda has been especially embraced by those ensconced in Puritan convictions seeing this agenda as embodying truly Christian values.

This is our roadmap for the next chapters. I want to try to find a way out of Jesus conservatism. But we need first to make the case for these conclusions. We start with our American predisposition to seeing religion in a Puritan way.

I

HOW WE GOT THE WAY WE ARE

1

The Puritan Paradigm

Several prominent scholars of American religion have contended that it is not possible to understand religious phenomena on U.S. soil apart from the recognition that much of what has happened and still happens in America is driven by a Puritan Paradigm.[1] I have already called attention to how many assumptions in the American social psyche are driven by Puritan ways of thinking, and continue to be even since the encroachment of German Enlightenment values on the masses since World War II. Later in the book, I'll provide some survey data to substantiate that point. Let's first get clear, though, on what the so-called Puritan Paradigm is and how it works.

We have already referred to this concept in the Introduction. Essentially, the Puritan Paradigm is the thesis that Puritanism has provided the primary categories for understanding American religiosity, that Americans themselves tend to understand religion—even their own religious convictions—in terms of these categories.

THE EMERGENCE OF PURITANISM: ITS CHARACTERISTICS

Puritanism is a late sixteenth–early seventeenth-century Protestant Movement originating in England. It was largely a reaction against the way the Reformation had gone in the sixteenth century in that kingdom. The Church of England that resulted was a disappointment to these Protestants, who were heavily influenced by the great Protestant Reformer John Calvin of Geneva. In the spirit of Calvin, they were more critical of Catholicism than Martin Luther or King Henry VIII and

11

Queen Elizabeth I had been. In fact, Henry and his daughter Elizabeth had retained much that was Catholic, like a Church governed by Bishops who claimed to be in line with the Apostles of Jesus, and a fixed, structured way of worship called the liturgy. (Consider how the Church of England's heir in America, The Episcopal Church, still retains some of these features.) At any rate, the Puritan agenda was above all to "purify" the Church of all vestiges of Roman Catholicism.

The Puritan Movement was a loose coalition. It included some moderate reformers willing to continue basic structures of the polity of the Anglican Church. But there were also radicals, totally opposed to maintaining the Office of Bishops in the Anglican Church on grounds that it was not Biblical. (These Puritans are the spiritual ancestors of today's Presbyterians, Congregationalists, and Baptists.)

After periods of persecution by the English royalty, Puritanism gradually impacted a group of increasingly influential citizens—the new class of capitalists. This was hardly surprising, given the fact that most scholars agree that the Puritans' spiritual father John Calvin was crucial in the development of the Protestant work ethic, with his stress on disciplined Christian living as a sign of one's election.[2] As time passed, Puritans grew more and more influential and actually began a revolution, which in 1649 successfully vanquished King Charles I and established a republic. It was forty years until the royal house was reestablished in England.

Why does it matter? The Mayflower Pilgrims who landed on American shores in 1620 were Puritans, who had earlier been banished from England in the period when Puritanism was just becoming a significant force under great suspicion by the king. These colonists and their ideas have had enormous influence on the American nation. More of that in a moment. First, let's get clear about what the early Puritans and the Pilgrims themselves believed.

Puritan Beliefs

During the era of the English republic, after King Charles I (1600–1649) had been beheaded, the British Parliament convened a meeting of Puritan leaders in Westminster, in order to clarify precisely what the "purified" Church of England should teach and practice. For our purposes the most crucial affirmations pertain to Biblical authority, predestination, Christian living, and church-state relations. These teachings are summarized in one of the most important church statements ever to reach American shores, *The Westminster Confession of Faith*.

Indebted to Calvin as they were, the Puritans gathered at this assembly clearly affirmed the sovereignty of God (V.1). With this was included a strong affirmation of election or predestination (III). To be a Puritan is to see oneself as part of an elect people. For all their preoccupation with freedom, belief in a sovereign God has continued to reflect in Americans' belief in their exceptionalism (the "chosen people" who live in the "promised land" in which God reigns over His Kingdom). Such a vision of God is no less evident today insofar as whenever a natural catastrophe occurs, the ensuing questions always reflect a belief that God is in control ("Why has God let this happen?" or "Why has God called her home?"), never the alternative that God's power is limited.[3]

A strong affirmation of Biblical authority was asserted (I). There is even one reference to "infallibility" in this section of the document (I.6). Whether the Westminster Puritans intended it or not, the legacy of the assembly in America has been an affirmation of an infallible Bible. Likewise, a passing reference they made to the unity of the Bible, to the oneness of its two covenants (the Old and New Testaments) "under various *dispensations*" (VII.6) has opened the way to theologies of Dispensationalism (a belief that in different eras God has acted differently) and a belief in the imminent end of the world evident in the popularity of Religious Right activist Tim LaHaye's *Left Behind* series of bestselling books. This construal of the Bible as infallible remains much alive today in America, as 2005 poll results by Barna Research reveal that a majority of women (66 percent) and of men (59 percent) believe the Bible is totally accurate in all its teachings.[4]

Other relevant Puritan affirmations included the reminder that even the faithful remain under the obligations of God's Law (XXI.5) and that the good works that ensue from obedience to these commandments "are the fruits and evidences of a true and lively faith" (XVIII.2). To be a Puritan is to live a life of assiduous obedience to what God has ordained, knowing that the work one does is a sign of faith and election. This sort of lifestyle certainly seems to nurture the ideal laborer for a growing capitalist economy.

Framers of *The Westminster Confession* clearly envisaged a role for Christian teachings in the affairs of state. Thus they claimed that the job of a civil magistrate is to protect the Church and to ensure that all the ordinances of God are observed (XXV.3). A task of government is to ensure that society reflects Christian principles. In fact, the Pilgrims who sailed to America on the Mayflower in 1620 believed that the new colony they were founding would "advance . . . the Christian religion" (as stated in the Mayflower Compact). At least by implication, a clear preference is implied in these commitments for government officials who are Christian. This is an additional Puritan commitment still reflected in polls of American voters.[5]

There is another dimension of early Puritanism, which is most relevant to today's political climate. We have already noted that the first Puritans largely drew their support from the English capitalists. A contemporary Puritan leader, Richard Baxter (1615–1691), even made this claim expressly.[6] Puritanism is quite evidently a version of Christianity that has been very friendly to capitalism and the free market.

The prevailing mercantilist economic system in England prior to the emergence of Puritan political power warrants attention. It had much in common with the Keynesian models of the old Democratic establishment's efforts to create the Great Society. Under the monarchy just before the Puritan Revolution, King Charles sought to nationalize industries, control foreign exchange, and to prosecute employers who did not pay fair wages and magistrates who did not give relief to the poor.[7]

Predictably in seeking to dismantle this sort of welfare net, the Puritans of the seventeenth century were not friendly to the poor. One of their later leaders, Richard Steele, wrote of idle beggars, warning the faithful not to spend "foolish pity upon their bodies, and . . . [urged] if more shewed some wise compassion upon their souls." Idleness was seen as the great evil and fault of the poor.[8] Puritans thought the poor were lazy. It sounds much like the assessment of poverty espoused by many members of the Republican majority today.

These attitudes were clearly transplanted to America by the first Puritans. One of the great American pulpit princes of nineteenth-century American Congregationalism (Puritanism), Henry Ward Beecher (1813–1887), the brother of the author of *Uncle Tom's Cabin*, looked at poverty this way:

> Looking comprehensively through city and town and village and country, the general truth will stand, that no man in this land suffers from poverty unless it be more that his fault—unless it be his sin . . . if men have not

enough, it is owing to the want of provident care, and foresight, and in-
dustry, and frugality, and wise saving.[9]

At other points we find a convergence between modern Republican
values and those of the Puritan leadership. Not unlike today, early Puritans, like Reverend Joseph Lee, came to regard the advancement of private persons as to the advantage of the public, and, another, Cotton
Mather, observed that as the Puritans *proceeded* in serving God they
"*prospered*" materially.[10] Michael Lerner does not have it quite right
when he claims that American mainline religion has been co-opted by
the Right as a result of American religion's fatalism that the world cannot be changed and by the technocratic rationality of our economic reality.[11] In fact, an intimate relation between the dominant strand of religion in America and the interests of the market is nothing new.
Puritanism, it seems, has always been a religion of the middle class and
the wealthy, and reflects their values.

IMPACT ON AMERICA

What does it all have to do with America and our present political
ethos? It is true that the Puritans were not the first Protestant group to
settle in North America. That honor belongs to The Church of England
in Virginia. But consider the deep impact of the Pilgrims (these early
Puritans) on American self-understanding.

The usual version of American history, dating back to public school
days (especially before multicultural sensitivity), was to begin with the
story of how "in fourteen-hundred, ninety-two, Columbus sailed the
ocean blue." It was then immediately followed with the story of the Pilgrims on the Mayflower and their subsequent settlement in New England. The later event is deeply embedded in American society, and has
been since Congress established a day of thanks in November 1863. As
much as anything, Thanksgiving is about the Pilgrim heritage (i.e., about
lionizing Puritanism).

In all sorts of ways, Puritanism has and continues to have an impact on
American life. Some of the oldest—and still most prestigious—American
churches are those First Congregational churches in the various cities and
towns of New England. Membership in those congregations does nothing
to hurt your social standing and business contacts. Likewise, in the South

it never hurts to belong to the town's First Baptist Church. And we must recognize here that the Baptist heritage itself is Puritan. The first Baptists were participants in the Puritan Movement in England. As a result, the first Baptist statements of faith embody most of the Puritan convictions we noted in *The Westminster Confession of Faith*.[12] Even if you did not grow up in such congregations, it is decidedly to your advantage economically, socially, and politically to belong to them.

Presbyterianism also had its origins in the Puritan Revolution of the seventeenth century. When we keep in mind the contributions to the American Revolution and the resulting Constitution of one of the first presidents of Princeton University, John Witherspoon (1723–1794), the relevance of Puritanism to the American system becomes immediately evident again. A Scottish-born Presbyterian pastor, Witherspoon was the only clergyman to sign the Declaration of Independence. But the plot thickens further when we notice the great influence he had on the secretary of the Constitutional Congress, James Madison. It is no accident that our system's separation of powers is based on the Puritan-like intuition that human beings are essentially selfish, always looking out for their own interests. Such an affirmation is also made clearly not just by Baron de Montesquieu [Charles-Louis de Secondat (1689–1755)], the eminent French intellectual who influenced many of America's Founders, but also by the Puritan *Westminster Confession of Faith*.[13] As Witherspoon once put it in a treatise on moral philosophy that may have been heard in lecture form by Madison while he studied at Princeton:

> Hence it appears that every good form of government must be complex, so that one principle may check the other. . . . it is folly to expect that a state should be upheld by integrity in all who have a share in managing it. They must be so balanced that when everyone draws to his own interest or inclination, there may be an over poise upon the whole.[14]

Of course even the representative democratic nature of the American system can be identified as Puritan in character. This sort of decision-making mechanism loosely follows the earlier Presbyterian form of church government, a denomination also rooted in Puritanism. Needless to say, we cannot overlook the fact that this was a Puritanism modified by the philosophy of Common Sense Realism and by the Deism embraced by several of the most prominent of America's Founders.[15] Their teaching of God as a mere clock maker has led most Americans to think of their democratic system more in terms of what we do, than as processes governed by the sovereign God, Who paradoxically is still deemed responsible for weather, births, and death.

We have already noted how certain specific congregations in New England and Baptist parishes in the South possess a certain prestige that other congregations identified with denominations rooted in the Puritan heritage do not. This pattern pertains to denominations themselves. To the list of Puritan-rooted denominations already noted (Presbyterians, Baptists, Congregationalists [at least in New England]), one should also add The Episcopal Church and The United Methodist Church. Although their origins are not directly rooted in Puritanism, both of the parents of John Wesley, the founder of the Methodist Movement, were raised in the Puritan ethos, so that much Reformed thinking is embedded in the Wesleyan heritage. Also noteworthy is that Puritanism originated in the Church of England and that many of the first Puritans remained loyal to that church.

It really is true, isn't it? The more your church connects with Puritan history and its theology, the more likely it is to be deemed socially acceptable. This is evident in that Jews, Roman Catholics, Pentecostals, historic African-American denominations, and Lutherans have never really been part of the American mainstream. After all, in centers of power, speaking in tongues, worshipping with a fixed liturgy, or handclapping and dancing in worship are not deemed characteristically American (or at least not socially acceptable) ways to do church. This manifests itself in the recognition that such styles of worship do not normally appear in prime-time television or in the movies when religion is presented (save for a few recent small-market cable TV reality shows). Far more likely when worship is portrayed empathetically, it is in the mode of a nonliturgical style, executed with sobriety. The pastor (the "reverend"—never a priest) is not dressed in traditional garb, but in coat and tie. The sermon, if shown, is rather sedately presented. Not much speaking in tongues, nor the emotive worship that characterizes the Black Church is portrayed in these media. Little wonder that Catholicism, Judaism, and even Islam have been regarded throughout their histories, until perhaps recently, as somewhat outside the American mainstream. Such dynamics are essential ingredients and prime manifestations of the Puritan Paradigm.

Given these dynamics it is hardly surprising that most American elites belong to the "truly American" churches of the Puritan Paradigm. Thus

George Bush is a Methodist raised in an Episcopalian home. The two previous Democratic Presidents were Baptists, and the front-runner at press time for the 2008 nomination, Hillary Clinton, is Methodist. The breakdown in Congress is much the same, with more Presbyterians and Episcopalians, along with Methodists and Baptists, on both sides of the Congressional aisles than members of every other religious persuasion. (Each of these denominations has a higher percentage of Congressional representation than its share of the American population). All of them are rooted in or related to the Puritan heritage. By contrast, we have had only one Catholic President, no Jews, no member of an African-American Church, and no Lutherans—all religious bodies not part of the Puritan Paradigm. Puritan-style religious life seems to help you politically. It can also help you do business, as the wealthiest Americans who are religious typically belong to the churches of the Puritan Paradigm.

Given these social pressures, it is not surprising that the Puritan ethos has had an impact on the adherents of other religious bodies like those already noted. Perhaps even against their wills, these religiously oriented Americans may begin to conform their communities ever so gradually to the prevailing attitudes until even people in churches with non-Puritan traditions begin to work and act like Puritans. Among the examples include the way in which segments of the American Jewish community have come to put more emphasis on Hanukkah than was typical in the Jewish tradition in the past as a result of the importance another December festival (Christmas) holds for parishioners of Puritan-Paradigm churches and other Americans. We can also observe these dynamics in operation in the diminution of liturgical worship and the infrequency of celebrations of the Sacrament of the Lord's Supper in certain non-Puritan traditions. American Lutheranism provides a good example. Its heritage does include these dimensions while sometimes de-emphasizing these practices in favor of the characteristically Puritan commitments to less structure in worship with more emphasis on preaching than on Sacraments. Like Jews, Lutherans wanted to become "American" (as defined by Puritanism). In some African-American churches, traditionally typified by a celebrative worship style, one experiences something like more characteristic of Puritan sobriety. The pressures on these religious groups are to conform to Puritan ways, because most Americans operate that way and especially the majority of those elites who remain religious.

CLOSING REFLECTIONS: WHAT IT ALL MEANS

The widespread impacts of Puritan ways of thinking and doing have obvious political consequences. The party or candidate who can tap into these sentiments stands a good chance of winning. A platform or message that reflects the mandates and values of Puritanism seems more likely to appeal to many Americans who are churchgoing (or even to those who do not, but who subscribe to Puritan views at least subliminally), than one that contradicts and ignores these Puritan convictions.

The analysis thus far may already have been sufficient to provide readers with a sense of the Bush, neoconservative electoral success. We have noted the pro-capitalist, even pro-bourgeois origins of Puritanism. Its early proponents were even inclined to blame the poor for their plight.

The small government, pro-business domestic policies of the Bush administration are just right for a Puritanized electorate. This Puritan Paradigm is a significant reason why the voices of religiously oriented prophets like Wallis, Press, Edgar, and Balmer, who try to make the case for a connection between Christian faith and actions on behalf of the poor, are not likely to have significant impact in the short-range future.

The relationship works both ways, to the advantage of all segments of the Neo-Conservative–Puritan coalition. As Max Weber long ago pointed out, the stress on discipline and works as a sign of election in Puritanism nurtures a good, trustworthy workforce for the CEOs and other entrepreneurs who have financially supported the President.

Recall the early Puritan vision of the role of the Christian ruler as assigned by God to ensure that God's ordinances are observed in society. The Republican coalition's articulated concerns about Christian values in the public sphere link it firmly with the American Puritan Paradigm. We see this especially when members of that coalition challenge Supreme Court rulings on school prayer and public displays of religion, and advocate religiously oriented alternatives to the teaching of Evolution in American public schools. The Neo-Conservative advocacy of teaching Intelligent Design Theory in public schools along with Evolution further links with early Puritanism's apparent affirmation of the Bible's infallibility.

It is evident how Republicans are embodying many of the values of the Puritan Paradigm. Given that paradigm's broad impact on the American social psyche, it's no wonder Republicans are winning elections.

2

Revivalism and the Privatizing of American Religion

Depending on what sort of reader you are, whether you have a general interest in politics and/or religion or are a scholar, and also depending on your religious affiliation, you will have a very different reaction to this chapter's title than your peers in another group. I venture to predict that most readers will either nod their heads in agreement or offer a polite, open-minded "could be." But at least some scholars of American religion, members of certain Holiness and historic African-American denominations might be ready for a fight. "What do you mean?" this core of readers is likely to say. "Early American revivalism, with its roots in Puritanism's the Great Awakening (1740–1745) and the Second Great Awakening (1795–1835), as well as much Black Church revivalism, have had strong social consciousness. Indeed, Revivalism in the Black Church has been about keeping alive the hope of liberation." At least to some extent, I will agree.[1]

When I refer to Revivalism in this book I am thinking about the way Billy Graham has popularized the concept, the way the average American hears the term. This sort of Revivalism is quite modern, owing to late nineteenth-century developments in earlier forms of American revivalism. Primary movers in these developments were the famed American Revivalists of the era, Dwight L. Moody (1837–1899) and William (Billy) Sunday (1862–1935), both of whom have strongly influenced Graham.[2]

Certainly the two Great Awakenings maintained a concern to change American society. A number of historians concur that the Great Awakening stimulated a sense of national consciousness in the Colonial era

of American history without which there would have been no successful Revolution. And the Second Great Awakening was in many ways
the mother of the Abolitionist Movement in the white community (even
the grandmother of modern Feminism). In this regard we can see that
early American Revivalism embodied the Puritan commitment to establishing a society governed by Christian principles. Jonathan Edwards (1703–1758), a Puritan Congregationalist who was one of the
great leaders of the Great Awakening, challenged the social structures
of his day with the Gospel (the nature of citizenship), urged that wealth
be shared with the poor, and pointed to the American experience as a
sign of the dawning of a more glorious day. In fact, this last observation reflected American Puritan beliefs that America and Americans
were clearly chosen by God as the location of His great works.[3] In view
of the impact of the Great Awakening on the formation of the American
republic, and given the revival's Puritan character, we can better understand how Puritan convictions have come to be so deeply embedded
in the American social psyche.

Social concern was no less a part of the Second Great Awakening. Although there is some debate about how publicly he did so, chief Revivalist of that later nineteenth-century Awakening Charles G. Finney
(1792–1875), himself nurtured in the Puritan heritage of Presbyterianism, condemned slavery. And a number of the leaders of the Women's
Suffrage Movement had their political initiation in the Abolitionist
Movement, which the Awakening mothered.[4] Revivals in this era that
led to the formation of the Holiness Movement were born of social concern about abolition and social class discrimination.[5]

REVIVALISM IN ITS MODERN FORM

Times have changed. Most Americans do not think of Revivalism as a
socially concerned phenomenon. This is not the way revivals are held
in most parts of American Protestantism today. Billy Graham's revivals
have never been about changing the American social structure. Revivals
are about "saving souls."

The crucial turning point in this evolution came after the Civil War,
a period of great social turbulence in America. In addition to the turbulence we normally associate with the era as a result of the agonies over

the reconstitution of the American Republic and over Reconstruction in the South, the American nation underwent a dizzying cultural change in the fifty years that followed the Civil War. The Industrial Revolution truly came to American shores, and with it came urbanization and a progressive ending of agrarian ways of life. New immigrants came in astoundingly high numbers—almost 22 million. Of these, less than 25 percent spoke English as their native tongue, many were not Protestant, and those who were did not belong to churches with historic or theological links to the dominant Puritan ethos of early America. For longtime American families, it was like they were losing their nation to the foreigners.

If the analogies between the feelings of late nineteenth-century Americans and today's late twentieth–early twenty-first century ethos are not already apparent, other points of similarity make the correspondence even more obvious. Not only were the new immigrants not like Americans in their cultural and religious attitudes. They kept on speaking those foreign languages in the communities and the businesses they built. (They seemed to prefer "their own kind.") As a son of immigrants, I refer here to the way average Americans viewed my grandparents, mother, and their generations.

These immigrants took the service jobs or those jobs in the factories that longtime Americans didn't want (except perhaps the rural poor who flocked into the cities). Most had been lower-class citizens of their homelands. Because of their background they were seen by some commentators as Europe's "moral and political refuse" who were a threat to national security.[6] Today's immigrants may come from different continents, but has much changed?

Eventually working conditions and the exploitation of the working classes by the new American capitalist elite brought about some reactions from the poorly-paid laborers, who originally had accepted these conditions because, bad as they were, they were still better than their previous lifestyles. At least there was more to do and enjoy in the city. And those sorts of temptations were leading to behaviors and religious practices that were not like the old days, when a rural version of the Puritan ethic along with Victorian morality still prevailed, at least among many parts of America east of the Appalachians. The churches in urban areas, still largely governed by practices and self-understandings that had worked better in small town and agrarian contexts, were not responding effectively to the increased social opportunities, drinking, and sex that city life afforded. American rural immigrants to the cities were not likely to check into the churches, and as for the immigrants, "they wanted their own [foreign] churches." Later as the nineteenth century proceeded, as the urban poor began to feel exploited in ways that the first wave of immigrants did not, labor organizations formed amidst much controversy. The disruptions that came with strikes as the century was closing suggested a kind of cultural upheaval that was unprecedented in American life, save the Civil War. Yes, America was changing, and for the average longtime American family, especially for those churchgoers who remained in the country or who had not let the city change their lifestyle, the fast-paced changes were not for the better.

Post-Bellum American Christianity needed a revival, it seemed. And the heritage of Charles Finney had produced plenty of Revivalists. In fact, thanks to Finney and his allies, revivals were a way of life in many congregations. But it took a New England–born Chicago businessman, Dwight Lyman Moody (1837–1899), to transform American Revivalism to address the new context. Though we might debate his success, there is no question about the attention his ministry was given in the English-speaking world and the impact he has had on Revivalist traditions in Protestantism.

Dwight L. Moody

We have already noted Moody's ongoing influence on his most famous successors, Billy Sunday and Billy Graham. His approach to the problems of his day would henceforth make Revivalism a movement about the individual born-again believer.

Born poor, with little formal education, Dwight Lyman Moody was a short, heavy-set man, blunt in dealing with people, but with a talent for friendship, highly energetic, and a great organizer. Unlike earlier Revivalists, he was the first to self-consciously employ the techniques of the growing business world to evangelism. Of course, this is not surprising given his business background in sales.

A successful shoe salesman, Moody's ministry began in Chicago by attracting urchins and drifters off the streets. After building his own church among the poor, the great evangelist began undertaking crusades in other locations, traveling even to England where he enjoyed as profound success as he ever achieved in the States. In short, Moody became the Billy Graham of his era.

Many of Moody's most significant supporters were rich, including John Wanamaker (founder of Wanamaker's Department Stores) and the wealthy Chicago real estate broker B. F. Jacobs. His supporters also included millionaires or business magnates Cyrus McCormick, George Armour, Arthur Tappan, Tappan's brother Lewis, and Moody's own brother-in-law Fleming Revell. These contacts had important implications for the Revivalist's fund-raising style. He typically obtained funds for his crusades by approaching prominent business leaders in the cities in which he operated.[7] This was a tradition that predated Moody, as the close ties between the revivals and the business establishment had been a modus operandi in American Christianity since the revivals of Charles G. Finney before the Civil War.

This link to business reflected in Moody's message. In ways suggestive of today's Prosperity Gospel (as embodied in media leaders like Joyce Meyer, T. D. Jakes, and Joel Osteen), Moody once claimed: "I don't see how a man can follow Christ and not be successful."[8] As already suggested, the relationship Moody nurtured between his revivals and the business establishment was really nothing new, but simply a way of further solidifying the link between capitalism and American religion bequeathed to America's churches by the Puritan Paradigm. Moody's brand of Christianity deeply resonated in the American [Puritan] social psyche. George Bush and the Neo-Conservatives pluck these same strings. Little wonder all have been perceived as advocating the "American way."

These were not isolated themes in the ministry of this famous evangelist. In an 1875 article entitled "The Workingman and His Foes," he wrote:

> Where the laws of God are obeyed and Christian morals prevail, there is also reciprocity of confidence and good-will; the workmen and their families are comfortable and contented and the proprietors prosperous.[9]

Some years later Moody took the logical implications of this affirmation to their conclusion and proceeded expressly to blame the poor for their poverty:

> I do not believe we would have these hard times if it had not been for sin and iniquity. Look at the money that is drank up! The money that is spent for tobacco![10]

Moody was only open to giving charity to the poor who deserved it. He and his associated institutions actually sought to combat "class hatred." There are even reports that some eminent Revivalists of the era like John Wilbur Chapman sent assistants to the factories to lure workers away from the influence of unions.[11] It sounds a lot like today's Neo-Conservative bombast against the poor and their warning against those who in defense of the poor resort to "class warfare"

Moody's overall theological perspective gives insights into his views on social ethics and also provides insight as to how his brand of Revivalism has transformed the Puritan Paradigm in America. The great Revivalist's message was a blend of American optimism and Evangelical Arminianism (the belief that to some extent our receptivity to God's love determines our eternal fate). In one of his sermons in a book characteristically titled *The Way to God and How to Find It* he underscores the point that we determine our eternal fate by our own choices.[12] This represents a clear break with the characteristically Puritan belief in a sovereign God Who determines all things. In holding these commitments, Moody along with his predecessor Finney and influential successors changed the American Puritan Paradigm, so that Americans are now more likely to think of their religion in terms of their own free will and what they can accomplish than in terms of a God Who determines all things.

This emphasis on individual responsibility led Moody to assert that public morality is improved through saving individuals in his view. As he once put it:

> A heart that is right with God and man seldom constitutes a social problem and by seeking first the kingdom and God and His righteousness nine-tenths of social betterment is effected by the convert himself.[13]

This is another conviction that has generally characterized American Revivalism and reshaped the Puritan Paradigm since Moody.

The heart of the Christian religion for Moody was the doctrine of the new birth. He makes this point expressly in an 1884 publication.[14] We already noted that the great Revivalist began his ministry among the poor with social action on their behalf. But later in his career he disowned this strategy on grounds that such social involvement led recipients to focus more on the material gifts given than on the Gospel and Christ, in direct contradiction to the Biblical witness.[15] This stress on being born again was a theme whose emphasis had earlier precedents in the history of American Revivalism in the ministry of Charles Finney. The theme remains central in all subsequent American Revivalism. But Moody also added reference to the Baptism of the Holy Ghost.[16]

We have already noted Moody's Arminianism and corresponding affirmation of free will. These commitments were also apparent in the earlier Revivalism of Finney. This optimism is of course in line with the American ethos, at least insofar as it is embodied in the Jeffersonian strand of American political theory.[17] The Revivalism of Moody and his heirs has tended to highlight this optimism to the relative neglect of the Puritan appreciation of our sinfulness. And yet there was also a pessimism in Moody, a belief that ultimately the world could not be improved, that only Christ's Second Coming could save the world from ruin. This premillennialist perspective contrasted with a kind of post-millennialism (the belief that first a golden age of peace and harmony would be created on earth as a prelude to Christ's Second Coming) that prevailed in the minds of earlier socially conscious Revivalists.[18]

The premillennialism moved Moody and his spiritual heirs to more pronounced advocacy of the separation of church and state, even to the point of not engaging the political realm at all in his crusades. This propensity surfaced in Moody's ministry in that he even practiced segregation in his Southern crusades.[19] And, of course, his general failure to place pressing social issues of his day in his preaching and writing, except to regard such issues as best addressed only by individuals assuming their responsibility for achieving the good life, further underlines this sociopolitical perspective.

Moody's premillennialism and the expectation of a catastrophic end of the world that he and other Revivalists transmitted to modern heirs like Tim LaHaye and Republican politicians the latter may have influenced is a logical development of Puritanism's apparent endorsement of Dispensationalism (*The Westminster Confession*, VII.6). In trying to argue for the "radical" character of American religion, and how its preoccupation with an imminent End Times is influencing the Republican machine, analysts like Kevin Phillips have it wrong in overlooking the Puritan roots of these convictions, how the Right's impact on American society is a function of tapping into the Puritan convictions that saturate American ways of thinking.[20]

Another way in which Moody resembles the Right today is evident in his views of the Theory of Evolution. As he once put it: "It is a great deal easier to believe that man was made after the image of God than to believe, as some young men and women are being taught now, that he is the offspring of a monkey."[21] The Religious Right of our day clearly walks in Moody's footsteps.

Despite his break with Puritanism in favor of free will, Moody's affirmation of a conservative view of Biblical authority, as well as his way of describing the Christian life and its associated political implications, remained in line with the Puritan Paradigm. The great Revivalist seems to have recognized this. Thus he once wrote: "I am an Arminian up to the Cross; after the Cross, a Calvinist."[22]

After Moody's death a controversy developed between those of his heritage and a new interest in relating faith to the challenging social issues of the day (evolving into the Social Gospel Movement). Leaders of the resistance to the social concern became leaders in the evolution of the Fundamentalist Movement. More on that in the next chapter. As we have noted, his impact lives on in the influence his methods of evangelism have had on Billy Sunday, Billy Graham, and their heirs.[23]

Billy Sunday

William (Billy) Sunday (1862–1935) was "Mr. Revivalist," the great popularizer of religion in America in the years prior to and during World War I. Moody may have standardized modern Revivalism, but Sunday firmly fixed and established this model. A major-league baseball star turned Presbyterian pastor and Revivalist, Sunday was a performer in the outfield and the pulpit. He brought his athleticism into the pulpit, where it was not uncommon to see him use pantomime, or to skip, run, or even slide on the stage, all the while drenched in his own perspiration. Not tall by today's standards, but athletic in build even after his playing days, Sunday was graced with a charming smile and a boyish, friendly nature. Without formal education, he was clearly a man of the people, and came to gear his preaching to the rough-and-tumble ways of the common man and woman of the early twentieth century. In today's vernacular, he was a man who "told it like it is," even if it took incorrect grammar and something less than elevated vocabulary.

Sunday's style was especially appropriate in his context. The beginning decades of the last century were a time when the old middle class (independent farmers, small businessmen, clerks, and other white-collar workers) was finding itself squeezed, as a business revolution that would transform America into an industrialized nation was progressing with more intensity than earlier in the years of Moody's ministry. A sense of the loss of American independence and self-reliance was in the air, along with a growing class distinction between rich and poor. The new factories were being manned by a new wave of immigrants who kept to themselves, worked for low wages (unless unionized), and sent money to their former homelands. (Have times changed much?)

In addition, the growing urbanization posed other challenges for the Church. A largely rural institution, the growth of the cities posed serious challenges for the Church. The situation was further exacerbated by the declining influence of Church leaders. With increased education of the professional classes, the clergy's corresponding declining influence was hardly surprising. Again the similarities between Sunday's era and our own are painfully obvious for Christians.

In this context, Sunday was both the antithesis of the mainline clergy and also very much a man of his times. In an era where big business called the shots, Sunday claimed business principles were central to his Revivalist work.[24] Not surprisingly, then, he was supported in his ministry by John D. Rockefeller.

The Moody heritage unambiguously reflects in Sunday's ministry and faith commitments in various ways. Much like his great nineteenth-century predecessor, Sunday affirmed free will and rejected the Theory of Evolution.[25]

Sunday's ministry especially appealed to upwardly mobile country-bred urban Americans of the era. He preached the Puritan values of thrift, stability, and hard work. His primary audience loved it, for he was affirming their lifestyle and values. As he once put it: "I never saw a Christian that was a hobo."[26] The modern Prosperity Gospel and its claim that God wants to bless the faithful with material well-being seems able to call on Sunday for precedents, and his ministry along with Moody's certainly sowed the seeds for its resonance among American Christians today. Indeed, this forerunner of our modern trends once even promised that women would get prettier the more they prayed![27]

It is hardly surprising given these commitments that the great Revivalist was regarded as a friend of business, and a critic of organized labor. True enough, he did lament poverty in some cases, but ultimately he insisted that a revival would change things.[28] Revivalism in America since Moody has not favored government solutions, but instead has taught us more lessons in individual responsibility.

Another core commitment of Sunday's revivals, most relevant for understanding our present political and religious climate, was his nationalism. This commitment even reflected in many of his altar calls. He frequently asked his revival audiences to give their hand "for God, for home, for my native land. . . ." As he put it in another sermon: "I think that Christianity and Patriotism are synonymous terms."[29] Salvation was basically a matter of decency, manliness, and patriotism. Of course a whole host of prominent evangelists of the era shared this commitment with him.[30]

Given these commitments and the Nativism (intolerance of foreigners) that characterized Sunday's early twentieth-century era, it is not surprising that we can identify in his ministry a kind of Puritan-like rigor about intolerance for diversity in America. In his view, the only foreigner worthy of acceptance as an American was "one who wants to come here and assimilate to our ways and conditions."[31] Revivalism and American Christianity have played significant roles in stimulating anti-immigrant attitudes ever since.

The key to becoming a "real" American for Sunday reveals more about how he shaped American Christian thinking for the rest of the twentieth century. The American is one who is a Bible-believing Protestant, is a "decent" middle-class citizen, and who has become a teetotaler.[32] The great Revivalist, much in the traditions of Puritanism and Methodism, supported and advocated for Prohibition. In his view, all the great social problems of the day were related to liquor. In fact in some of his crusades, the Prohibition theme was featured. Such support was not given by Sunday to the labor union movement even though management-labor relations were tense in his day and times.

In fact, Sunday even claimed "you can't legislate men out of the slough of despond."[33] Of course, this is hardly surprising given the support of big business that Sunday's crusades enjoyed. Dwight Moody and Billy Sunday solidified the modern Revivalist continuation of the Puritan Paradigm's bias toward business interests over labor. In view of the role of Puritanism in defining American religiosity, it is all the more clear how George Bush and his allies could conduct their pro-business policies in the name of Jesus. These trends have been even more deeply ensconced in the American social psyche through the ministry of Billy Graham.

Billy Graham to the Present

Revivalism began to receive bad press as the early twentieth century proceeded. Some of it had to do with the discrediting of Fundamentalism after the Scopes Trial (the famed "Monkey Trial") over the teaching of Evolution in our public schools. More on that in the next chapter. In any case, some of the reasons for the loss of credibility by Revivalism had to do with a sense that its leaders were not preaching or advocating a cultured, sophisticated religion. Consequently, until Billy Graham burst on the American and international scene, Revivalism only continued to flourish among Holiness and Pentecostal churches or others whose constituencies were comprised of those with little formal education, a core group of the Right's constituency today.[34]

William Franklin Graham (b. 1918) is an icon of American religion. His personal magnetism and decency have attracted a worldwide following. His success has also been a function of the media (he burst into prominence in his 1949 Los Angeles Revival when William Randolph Hearst of the Hearst newspaper empire ordered his editors to "puff Graham"), as well as of the rebirth of Christian theological conservatism (the emergence of the Evangelical Movement out of a largely discredited, demoralized Fundamentalism). Not only has he generally borrowed the revival techniques of Moody and Sunday, bringing them into the media age, but he also endorses many of their other themes pertinent to the interplay of Christianity and politics.

The litany is by now familiar. Graham has shared Sunday's nationalism, speaking in 1955 of how, "If you would be a true patriot, then become a Christian." A year later he spoke of America's "God-appointed mission," to function as the "last bulwark of Christian Civilization" against Communism.[35] In the midst of all the cynicism of the late 1960s he was speaking positively of the government we are to honor.[36]

Graham seldom condemns social sins. In fact, no less a prominent analyst of American religion than Reinhold Niebuhr proposed that Graham was not making his converts see their duty as seeking justice in society, but was merely concentrating on overcoming personal sin.[37] Graham himself has confirmed Niebuhr's analysis of the evangelist's priorities. Speaking in 1974 before an international audience he claimed, "Let us rejoice in social action and yet insist that it alone is not evangelism, and cannot be substituted for evangelism." In part, this was a matter of strategy, for he has claimed that before we can change society we must change man.[38]

This priority on converting believers as the key to social change, and the corresponding conviction that small government is the best government, has evidenced itself in Graham's treatments of race and poverty. In his famous 1957 New York Crusade he claimed that "The one great answer to our racial problem in America is for men and women to be converted to Christ." In other contexts he has asserted that love and the spirit of Jesus are what we need to overcome poverty.[39]

Graham's personal record on race has been similarly unclear. The standard line has been that he was ahead of the country, integrating his crusades even in the South as early as 1953. Others contend, however, that his earlier revivals in that region had been conducted with segregated seating, and that he only integrated his meetings after the 1954 Supreme Court ruling on integrating public schools.[40] At least with regard to issues associated with liberalism, Billy Graham seems to embody a Christianity that does not agitate for justice, but obeys the laws of the land.

There are other ways in which Graham's ministry has set in motion trends that prefigure what is happening in our public life today. Just as Sunday prefigured today's Prosperity Gospel, so Graham, most notably in a sermon entitled "Partners with God," has proclaimed themes suggesting that faith in God will lead to material blessings. After asserting that if a man went "in business with God" by becoming a good steward and tithing his income, he could double or triple his income, the great Evangelist asserted: "You cannot get around it, the Scripture promises material and spiritual benefits to the man who gives to God."[41]

Graham's prioritizing of evangelism over social action and politics has not negated the Puritanism of his orientation, much of it perhaps embedded in his spiritual psyche from his Presbyterian upbringing. For example, in line with the Puritan conviction that our politics should be ruled by Christian principles, Graham has claimed that without love Christian social concern is empty.[42] This perspective has also carried with it the historic Puritan biases we have observed in favor of free-market capitalism. Thus Graham has been on record making veiled attacks on various New Deal, big-government policies. He has also spoken of "Capitalist America" and urged that we must remain "devoted to the individualism that made America great." He has even gone so far as to contend that such a spirit of free enterprise is indebted to the Puritan heritage of America.[43]

Quite significant for our interests has been Graham's early vision of a political movement of Conservative Evangelicals. In a 1952 speech delivered to the Convention of the National Association of Evangelicals, long before Jerry Falwell and the Moral Majority, Graham claimed: "In the coming election there's going to be the Jewish bloc, the Roman Catholic bloc, there's going to be the labor bloc. . . . Why should not Evangelicals across America be conditioned and cultured and instructed until we, too, can make our voice known?"[44] Billy Graham's ministry prefigures many of the developments of the modern Religious Right. His popularity—the popularity of his vision of Christian faith—helps explain how the New Right, by invoking these themes, could gain the popularity and influence it has today.

HOW REVIVALISM CHANGED THE
PURITAN PARADIGM FOR A SECULARIST AGE

The Puritan ethos is still largely in place, even after Modern Revivalism altered the characteristic American spirituality. Although the newer form of Revivalism nudged the American Church out of politics as it focused spirituality on the individual's piety, we have seen that it did not alter the Puritan conviction that Christians make the best citizens and that Christian values have a place in guiding American political institutions.[45] Revivalism also seems to embody the Puritan preference for capitalist dynamics, as even Billy Graham has noticed. To be sure, Modern Revivalism's Arminian, freewill orientation challenged the Puritan commitment to the sovereignty of God and the belief that only God can work good. This aspect of Revivalism (its teaching of free will and the corresponding possibility that we can make ourselves good, to the relative neglect of the Puritan insistence on our sinfulness) found such resonance in the American social psyche precisely because it connected with the Founders' stress on freedom and their Deism.[46]

No two ways about it, the Modern Revivalist affirmation of our freedom has to some extent supplanted Puritan preoccupation with strong affirmations of divine providence and predestination. This displacement of the sovereign God created a certain flexibility in the American Puritan outlook to allow it to be adopted more readily by Secularists. With the sovereign God replaced by an Arminian God who allows for human contributions, these Americans could now share the Puritan commitment to American exceptionalism and the promise of a good life for those living Puritan capitalist values, now seen as established not by God and Biblical principles, which had been pushed aside, but by science and progress.[47] Of course, as previously noted, this whole process had precedents in the previous century with the coalition between Puritans and Enlightenment Deists in the formation of the American Republic.

Nevertheless, despite these Revivalist amendments to the Puritan heritage, a conviction about divine sovereignty remains strongly present in the American social psyche, side-by-side with the Revivalist-Deist affirmation of human freedom. The theme of divine sovereignty still seems alive and well to the extent that the Constitution's conviction about the need to limit human power remains in place.[48] It also remains and is well to the extent that when natural catastrophes strike, commentators inevitably question religious adherents and receive answers presupposing that God is in charge of nature (a strong doctrine of Providence, most suggestive of Puritan convictions). Whenever politicians can tap into these and other theological convictions pertaining to discipline in the Christian life, as well as into the de-emphasis on ritual that characterizes American Puritanism modified by Revivalism, as the Right has done so successfully, it will also strike a deep resonance in the social psyche of most Americans.

3

Fundamentalism, Its Decline, and the Rise of the Religious Right

The failure of the Moody and Sunday revivals to bring about an awakening in America, to reverse the negative side effects of urbanization, industrialization, and immigration drove Christians associated with Revivalism into a kind of exile. No longer did they have media support. They tended more and more to cluster in the newer, "less respectable" denominations like Holiness and newer Pentecostal churches, or in independent congregations.[1] Gradually this segment of American Christianity came to identify itself with the Fundamentalist Movement. Revivalism's new partner had emerged earlier in the twentieth century among other segments of the theologically conservative of the American church put off by many of the same social dynamics with which Revivalism had grappled. Fundamentalism had also developed in response to consternation about the new scientific and historical scholarship flourishing in elite circles.[2]

The other, older strands that comprised Fundamentalism were unambiguously Puritan in theological profile. One segment was comprised of a group of conservative Presbyterians and Baptists interested in speculations about the End Times. They convened various Bible and Prophetic Conferences during the last two decades of the nineteenth century. They largely shared Dwight Moody's and Billy Sunday's pessimism about the future, as they opted for a premillennialist perspective (believing that the world must get worse before the Church returns). The premillennialism was typically mixed with a belief in Dispensationalism.[3]

The other segment that created Fundamentalism was an exclusive strand rooted in the Ivy League. Leaders of Princeton Seminary represented a very conservative brand of Presbyterianism (the Old School, which embodied a Reformed piety most compatible with older Puritan assumptions) that had dominated the seminary's campus since its early nineteenth-century founding by Archibald Alexander (1772–1851). Under his eminent successors, especially B. B. Warfield (1851–1921) and J. Gresham Machen (1881–1937), Princeton Theology became a bastion for resisting efforts to use new insights about history and new scientific insights like the Theory of Evolution.

Influential as they were, it is not surprising that the main proponents of Princeton Theology succeeded in getting their denomination to accept in 1910 the Five-Point Deliverance, which echoed the Princetonians' earlier claim that the very words of Scripture are inspired, totally inspired, and that Scripture will not be proven to err even with respect to science and history.[4] This affirmation was effectively a robust affirmation of the conservative view of Scripture of the denomination's roots.

Several proponents of Princeton Theology (though not the Princeton theologians themselves) began attending the Bible and Prophetic Conferences. Gradually, the participants of these conferences came to endorse Princeton Theology's view of the Biblical authority as articulating what they believed in a scholarly forum. Though not all participants in these late nineteenth-century gatherings came from traditions affirming Biblical inerrancy, Princeton Theology's impact opened the way for more Baptists and Methodists, conservative Episcopalians and Congregationalists, as well as Holiness Christians to begin employing the terminology. Later in his career, Princeton Theologian J. Gresham Machen even participated in a Revivalist Bible conference. In view of the Revivalists' and the Bible–Prophetic Conference constituency's growing identification with Princeton Theology and its adherents, the stage was set for a movement of nationwide significance. But, as we have seen, it was a movement predicated on American Puritan assumptions tempered by Revivalism, whose political suppositions were pro–free market and pro-business. The Princetonian stress on divine sovereignty led some of its leaders to make comments that were readily interpreted by some as rejections of Abolition and Women's Suffrage.[5] This sociopolitical conservatism was also characteristic of Revivalism since Moody further strengthened the pro–free market, small-government commitments of the coalition that would emerge.

THE FORMATION OF THE FUNDAMENTALIST MOVEMENT

A crucial turning point in the formation of the Fundamentalist Movement was the publication between 1910 and 1915 of a series of well-known booklets that were widely distributed to clergy, theological students, and church workers across the nation. Titled *The Fundamentals*, the series was funded by oil millionaire Lyman Stewart and another rich colleague who recruited theologically conservative editors to provide "a new statement of the fundamentals of Christianity" in this time when these fundamentals were obviously under fire.[6] The immediate reaction was not nationally significant, but it made a deep imprint on the conservative core receiving the booklets. It became a point of reference for the new coalition that formed after the completion of World War I.

With the completion of the war, America as a whole and its Christian citizens faced even more intense anxieties. Not only were the late nineteenth-century trends of industrialization, immigration, and secularization continuing, Enlightenment historicism and the Theory of Evolution were beginning to permeate the American educational curriculum, even in its seminaries and national church leadership. But the war had brought a sense of isolationism to America, including a revival of anti-immigrant sentiment. All this was further exacerbated by a growing fear of Communism called the "Red Scare."

The years just prior to the roaring twenties and in that decade were not a good time for organized labor. Also with the 1920s on the horizon, this was seen as an era of growing moral indiscretion. Smoking was now done in public. Women, just recently given the franchise, bared themselves. Dancing, once forbidden, was widely accepted. About all the Church had to celebrate, it seemed, was the adoption of the Prohibition Amendment.

The growing sense of crisis clearly contributed to the formal organizing of the emerging coalition of theological conservatives, which finally transpired in 1919 with the formation of the World's Christian Fundamentals Association. Emboldened by political successes like the passage of the Prohibition Amendment, their intended purpose was to save America. Key leaders were a conservative Baptist associated with the Bible and Prophetic Conference Movement and a significant representative of the Moody heritage and the Revivalist Movement, William B. Riley (1861–1947) and R. A. Torrey (1865–1928). Conservative Presbyterians were increasingly drawn into the orbit of these leaders, hardly surprising given the emerging Fundamentalism's reliance on the theological suppositions of Princeton Theology. The Fundamentalist cause gained further stature when the eminent Princeton professor J. Gresham Machen identified himself with the Movement.

THE RISE AND FALL OF THE MOVEMENT

The inclusion of Presbyterians and sophisticated Ivy League faculty, as well as the temper of the times, led Fundamentalism to become a media darling. In fact, the name of the Movement, "Fundamentalism," was the creation of the media.[7] In its origins, then, at least its leading spokesmen were educated white Protestants from north of the Mason-Dixon Line (hardly the image most Americans have of the Movement today).[8] Of course there was a natural affinity that working-class religious conservatives in America had with the Movement. The constituency eventually broadened to the South as a result of the Fundamentalist efforts to "save" the schools. The heritage of Princeton Theology's sociopolitical conservatism, the sort that would not challenge segregation, entailed that the Fundamentalist embrace of Princeton theological suppositions gave the Movement more credibility in a Southern white ethos. (At this time, though, most white Southern Protestants did not need a Fundamentalist Movement because their denominations were largely under theologically conservative leadership.)

The way to save America, the new coalition concluded, was to win back the churches (Northern-based denominations) from Liberalism and win back American culture and its schools from antibiblical intellectual developments. The battle for the churches primarily focused on three Northern denominations all coming under the sway of Liberal Theology—the Northern Baptist Convention, the Presbyterian Church in the U.S.A., and the Disciples of Christ. (It is interesting to note that all three have Puritan roots.) Efforts by Fundamentalists to take over these denominations in the second half of the 1920s ultimately failed. These efforts did win more media exposure for the Fundamentalist cause. Besides, the Movement's Puritan orientation resonated deeply with the American social psyche. But it gained further nationwide attention in its struggle to win back American culture through a crusade against the Theory of Evolution.

The Theory of Evolution had become a symbol for the Fundamentalists of all that was wrong with America. It is interesting to note that sometimes Darwinism was seen by the conservatives as the philosophy that epitomized prewar German culture, so that their anti-Evolutionary stance and their polemic against German forms of Liberal Theology should be seen in relation to the anti-German sentiment in America during the war. It was in its effort to purge American society of Evolutionary Theory that the Fundamentalist Movement truly became a national movement.

The active involvement in the anti-Evolutionary cause of (three-time candidate for the presidency of the United States) William Jennings Bryan (1860–1925) gave the entire Fundamentalist cause a new prominence. The new exposure broadened the base of the conservatives' support in the South, so that while the Fundamentalist premillennialist movement had been to that time only a concern in the North, by 1920 it was attracting national interest.

It is true that the Secular media were principally interested in the anti-Evolutionist position of the Fundamentalists and not so much in the broad range of their doctrinal and political concerns. But many members of the emerging Movement seemed to recognize that by giving heightened attention to the problem of Evolutionary Theory as the Movement did, they could appeal to a broader constituency. In that way the Movement's overall concern to call back the churches and American society would receive a broader hearing.[9] In a sense, history seems to be repeating in our context today. No doubt this dynamic accounts in part for the deep impression the Fundamentalist Movement as a whole made on American society in the 1920s and continues to make.

The Scopes Trial and Its Aftermath

By the mid-1920s Fundamentalism had experienced or was about to experience several humiliating defeats. It had failed in its efforts to take over the Northern denominations it had targeted, and its leaders in these denominations had been marginalized, with some seceding to form Fundamentalist versions of their old denominations. It was the Scopes Trial of 1925 that placed the Movement's prestige on the line. Fundamentalism's subsequent humiliation and retreat into a kind of ghetto for nearly five decades was to a great extent a function of its humiliation in this court case.

The story is familiar, but warrants a brief reiteration. Efforts by Fundamentalist-related organizations to legislate against teaching Evolution in the schools succeeded in several states. In 1923, Oklahoma became the first state to pass legislation to implement such a ban. Other Southern states followed, including Tennessee in 1925. The stage was set for the first test of the legislation that year in Dayton, Tennessee.

Almost immediately after the law was signed, a young high school biology teacher, John T. Scopes, was indicted for teaching Evolution in violation of the law. By this time the anti-Evolution Movement had obtained so much publicity and marshaled so many resources that a backlash was emerging. The American Civil Liberties Union (ACLU) led this backlash and announced that it would finance a test case to challenge the constitutionality of the Tennessee law. There is some evidence that Scopes volunteered to undertake this challenge. The most famous American criminal lawyer of the time, and an opponent of organized religion, Clarence Darrow (1857–1938), volunteered his services to help the defense. William Jennings Bryan, who had been heavily involved in the anti-Evolution Movement and was personally associated with Fundamentalism, volunteered to help the prosecution.

The outcome and the trial (Scopes was found guilty, but the verdict was later reversed on a technicality) was not nearly as important to American society as what the media made of the event. And the trial was indeed a "media event." In view of the great interest and fears that had been aroused by the anti-Evolutionists Dayton was packed with more than one hundred reporters to cover the "Monkey Trial." By their account, the high point of the trial came when Darrow cross-examined Bryan, who was testifying as an expert witness. Bryan and his Fundamentalist views were made to look very bad, quite naive and uncultured, by Darrow's ruthless interrogation. It was as if Bryan were incapable of answering village-atheist challenges to the Bible's authority.[10] He died in Dayton, a broken man, not long after the trial ended.

The press portrayed the trial, this exchange, and the quite obviously pro-Fundamentalist stance of the Dayton population in such a way that not only Bryan but also those associated with him were made to appear to readers as mindless bigots, opposed to all that was intellectually respectable, and largely rural or "Southern" in mentality.[11] In short, many of the false stereotypes of Fundamentalism, stereotypes that I have already challenged in this analysis, have their original source in press coverage of the Scopes Trial.

The brutal press coverage of the trial spelled the end of Fundamentalism's popular support, at least in the centers of American power and influence. Indeed, given their new media image, it is hardly surprising that Fundamentalists failed in their efforts to take control of the major American denominations. They were no longer perceived as representing an identifiable Protestant consensus. Moderates in their churches or in society who might otherwise have shared the Fundamentalist critique of theological liberalism and certain sociopolitical developments in American society would no longer wish to be associated with the Movement, which by now was being perceived as representing anti-intellectualism and strictly rural interests. This image was somewhat reinforced by the sectarian, anti-intellectual, unsophisticated atmosphere associated with the crusades of Billy Sunday, who became the rallying point of many of the faithful Fundamentalist few after the Scopes Trial. Nor was this helped by scandals involving two of Fundamentalism's most prominent leaders, Frank Norris and T. T. Shields.

FUNDAMENTALIST DECLINE AND RENEWAL

With its image firmly fixed in the press and in the minds of most Americans, the press and academia soon lost interest in Fundamentalism by the 1930s. Given its negative image and the apparent hopelessness of its influencing American society and its churches, it is hardly surprising that retreat into the ghetto seemed to be the only option. Thus Fundamentalists intensified their work in forming more of their own educational institutions (Bible Schools), mission organizations, and denominations. In addition to the precedents that already existed for forming their own institutions, such developments were also quite logical in view of the separatist tendencies and the premillennialist perspective of the earlier Fundamentalism.

This orientation also tended to encourage political detachment on the part of the Fundamentalist Movement, since Western society was thought to be on its way to destruction in any case. Political intervention on the part of the Fundamentalists was likewise discouraged by their equation of such activity with the Social Gospel Movement, which they perhaps unfairly equated with Liberal Theology. When political positions were taken, they were largely conservative, in accord with the Victorian and pro-capitalist Puritan and Revivalist origins of the Fundamentalist Movement. Given such an orientation, any political alternative presenting itself as liberal, as calling for change, quite naturally appeared to bury the antebellum Puritan values deeper in the past and so had to be opposed.[12]

The Fundamentalist retreat into a kind of ghetto and creation of its own subculture with its own institutions has rendered the Movement a kind of "cognitive minority." That is, its members may perceive themselves to be a minority in relation to the broad culture. The imposition of certain behavioral norms, like strict, pleasure-denying lifestyle standards, has sometimes also served to heighten this minority syndrome and to strengthen the Movement against cultural accommodation.

This sense of being a cognitive minority most certainly also pertains to Fundamentalism's spiritual heir, the Evangelical Movement. Insofar as these two strands of theological conservatism comprise much of the Religious Right, we can better understand the Right's own self-understanding today as a castigated minority, despite the power it has wielded since the Reagan Revolution.

The Fundamentalist Renaissance

The development of this subculture during the years of retreat since 1925 clearly had unwitting positive effects on the Movement that have also made possible the Religious Right's emergence as a political force. The subculture that emerged, with its unique values and institutions, helped Fundamentalists preserve their beliefs and their vision during the following decades of flux and the relativizing of values. This mentality and their premillennialist worldview made them especially well-prepared to cope with the Depression of the 1930s and the Second World War, which followed.[13]

The premillennial commitments did not negate Fundamentalism's other convictions. Consequently, even in this period of withdrawal, through its Revivalist strands Fundamentalism was not devoid of a concern with evangelism. In fact, the years prior to World War II were a period of numerical growth. This growth came both in terms of converts and also in virtue of broadening the Fundamentalist coalition. For example, during the period before World War II, some denominations with a strong Pietist bent that had retained an ethnic background (like the Evangelical Covenant Church and the Evangelical Free Church), Holiness and Pentecostal churches (such as The Wesleyan Church and the Assemblies of God), some Mennonite churches, as well as segments of mainline Baptist, Presbyterian, and Methodist denominations in the South, came more and more under Fundamentalist influence.

Fundamentalist growth in this period was also related to the beginnings the Movement made in the use of the media for evangelism. Among the most notable examples were the "Old-Fashioned Revival Hour" of Charles Fuller (1887–1968) and a CBS network Christian broadcast hosted by Donald Grey Barnhouse (1895–1960). Fundamentalism was anything but dead, as its critics asserted in this period. The Movement even experienced growth in respect to its para-church agencies, including its schools.[14]

Another Fundamentalist commitment of long standing, which was not completely forfeited after 1925, was the old Puritan concern with preserving the foundations of American society by means of restoring their Christian character. Consequently, the Fundamentalists' nationalistic attitudes were maintained, even intensified, during and after World War II. This manifested itself in the 1950s in the strident anti-Communism of Billy James Hargis (1925–2004) and the American Council of Christian Churches led by Carl McIntire (1906–2002). Bob Jones Sr. (1883–1968) joined these voices during these years and even earlier, adding a strident Southern Democratic perspective on racial segregation to the mix.[15]

The growth and new ventures of the Fundamentalist Movement after the mid-1920s had the unwitting effect of opening it to wider cultural influences, despite its avowed separatism. These factors, plus the upward social mobility of some Fundamentalists, led to a certain discontent with the "sectarianism" of their heritage. This in turn made possible a climate that permitted a few to receive theological education in prestigious academic settings, a development that further contributed to setting the stage for the emergence of the Evangelical Movement during World War II.

Although the emergence of the Evangelical Movement, to which we have already alluded, effectively removed many former Fundamentalists from the Fundamentalist Movement, the latter has continued to flourish since the Second World War. The 1950s and 1960s were times of great numerical growth for churches affiliated with both movements. And as we are already aware, Fundamentalism has had no little political and cultural impact on America since the 1970s with the rise of the Moral Majority and its successor organizations, each attempting in its own way to reinstall Christian values in American society.

The rejuvenation of Fundamentalism suggests the truth of my core insight about American religion. When the old-time religion (a conservative Protestant faith perspective, a mixture of Puritan and revivalist themes) is yoked with a concern to "Christianize" the structures of American society, it seems to tap into the deepest roots of the American social psyche. American religion (and politics) best succeeds when it can lay claim (in the minds of constituents and the general public) to be the bearer of the American Puritan heritage.

THE EMERGENCE OF THE EVANGELICAL MOVEMENT AND THE RELIGIOUS RIGHT

Despite the organized interpenetration of the Evangelical Movement and Fundamentalism, they are not identical. The Evangelical Movement, the largest segment of the Religious Right, actually did not emerge until the 1940s. Rooted in the Fundamentalist heritage, we might describe it as "Fundamentalist-lite." For the separatist tendencies of Fundamentalism have largely been repudiated by this newer Movement.

We previously noted the emergence of the Evangelical Movement through the leadership of Harold Ockenga (1905–1985) and various younger Fundamentalist colleagues distraught over the Movement's cultic, increasingly anti-intellectual character and failures after the Scopes Trial debacle. Armed in many cases by superior theological education in non-Fundamentalist institutions, these early leaders proposed that the task of their Movement should be to "infiltrate rather than separate" from liberal church leaders, to package the fundamentals of the faith in more appealing, inclusive, and politically relevant ways than their immediate predecessors had.[16] The landmark event in the development of the nascent Movement was the establishment of the *National Association of Evangelicals* in 1942, a cooperative organization that emerged from an earlier predecessor, the New England Fellowship founded by J. Elwin Wright (1896–1966).

The decision to use the term "Evangelical" rather than "Fundamentalist" for the new Movement was a deliberate one. Most observers give Ockenga credit for the new designation, and he has claimed credit for it. The new Movement was to identify itself with older antebellum Protestant Evangelicalism. Implicit in this claim was that only those American Christians who affirm the old Fundamentals of this faith could truly lay claim to the most venerable and authentic traditions of American Christianity (its Puritan and Revivalist roots).[17] The media and the general public have largely been converted to this way of thinking, so that mainline Protestant churches, even those with "Evangelical" in their corporate titles, are rarely counted as "Evangelical."

Another dimension of the origins of the National Association of Evangelicals and the Evangelical Movement was that it inherited from its Fundamentalist (and therefore from its Puritan) roots an anti-Communism and a critical perspective on the social engineering approaches of the New Deal.[18] These aspects of Evangelical origins continue to influence the politics of the Religious Right, which has emerged from this constituency. Again and again, as we observe how many of the Religious Right's present political commitments are rooted in the heritage of its predominant institutions, it becomes apparent why political machines that espouse these views can readily market them to theologically conservative Christians, passing such policies off as Christ's Way. Little wonder that Jesus seems conservative to so many American Christians.

Billy Graham has also been a major leader in the Movement, to the point that sometimes the Evangelicals have been identified as "those who connected with organizations founded by Billy Graham or on which he serves as a trustee."[19] Among the most important of these organizations for the American scene have been *Christianity Today*, Fuller Seminary, and Campus Crusade. He has also founded or sponsored various foreign and domestic missionary organizations associated with the

Evangelical Movement. The early histories of these premiere Evangelical organizations and Graham's own political dispositions provide us with significant glimpses of the foundational political preferences of the Evangelical constituency today, commitments that the Republican Party has so successfully exploited.

Premiere Evangelical Institutions and Associated Political Aims

Of course, we cannot think of Billy Graham and the Evangelical Movement apart from the organization he founded in 1950 to support his Crusades, the Billy Graham Evangelistic Association. Graham and his family were the driving force in the founding of *Christianity Today*, which has become the Movement's premiere Christian magazine. Its founding editor, Carl F. H. Henry (1913–2003), was recognized as the premiere theologian of conservative Evangelicalism until his death. His immediate successor, Harold Lindsell (1913–1998), kept the periodical firmly within the orbit of the most conservative elements of the Evangelical coalition, albeit in a more strident way.

Graham has also been a member of the Board of Trustees of the Evangelical Movement's flagship institution of theological education, Fuller Seminary. Founded in 1947 by Harold Ockenga and the famous radio preacher Charles Fuller, their intention was to establish an institution of the highest academic caliber for the Movement. It assembled a fine faculty of young scholars who, like Carl Henry, became the first generation of theological leaders of the new Movement. Although the faculty's openness to new ideas and willingness to engage in dialogue with mainline theological trends has been a source of some controversy in the more theologically conservative segments of the Evangelical Movement, the reputation of the school as the place for training the Movement's leaders for the next generation remains unimpaired.[20] Also noteworthy is Graham's alma mater, Wheaton College, a theologically conservative undergraduate institution founded in 1860 in the Chicago area.

Graham's own ministry began with his service in a youth ministry organization called Youth for Christ. Founded in 1943 by Pentecostal pastor Roger Malsbary, the organization was supported by various members of the business establishment in the Midwest. It received nationwide publicity from newspaper mogul William Randolph Hearst, who later came to "puff" Graham to fame. After organizing in 1945, the organization became international under the leadership of Reverend Torrey Johnson (1909–2002), an early leader in the Evangelical Movement who mentored Graham and later recruited him for the organization during the latter's years as a student at Wheaton College.

A parallel youth ministry organization that has become even larger and more influential over the years has been Campus Crusade. Founded in 1951 by a Presbyterian layman, Bill Bright (1921–2003), the ministry has grown to 1,100 college campuses in the United States with a staff of 26,000 worldwide. Targeting college campuses, the ministry has spread to providing church-growth models for congregations.

Billy Graham's influence on the Evangelical Movement is not just evident in his spiritual and institutional leadership. In many ways his political orientation typifies the main strands of the Movement and prefigures the Religious Right's policies today. We have already noted in the last chapter that, although he has seen his ministry as one of an evangelist, not as a social activist, he still envisioned the formation of an Evangelical voting bloc as early as 1952 at the Annual Convention of the National Association of Evangelicals. Likewise, we have already observed his Revivalist-Puritan bias toward the free market and related critiques of the managed-market strategies of Democrats since the Roosevelt era. So permeated has Graham's ministry been with business models, not unlike his famous Revivalist forebears, that he has spoken of his ministry in terms of business models, as "selling the greatest product in the earth."[21] Linked to these convictions are his affirmations of "rugged individualism," which he claimed, at least once while speaking in Greensboro, North Carolina, "that Christ bought," a nationalism that envisions America as the last bulwark of civilization against Communism.

Granted, as we have noted, the great Evangelist did integrate his Crusades (eventually) and seemed to have some general sympathy with the War on Poverty of his longtime acquaintance Lyndon Johnson. In each case, though, he shied away from making specific recommendations.[22] Such a posture is very much in line with the small-government posture of the modern Republican Party.

These convictions more or less reflected in the first theological leaders of the Evangelical Movement. Carl Henry, as founding editor of the leading media outlet, the Graham-inspired *Christianity Today*, played a significant role in awakening conservative American Christianity to social concern, at least making it respectable. But his cautiousness, though radical in its context, came to receive criticism of moderate to liberal Evangelicals since the 1960s, like Jim Wallis and Ron Sider. His politics were clearly more Republican, on such issues as Women's Liberation and government aid for the poor.[23] All this was done with a Puritan-like awareness that all realms of human life, including economics and politics, must be governed by distinct Christian principles. Thus Henry wrote in 1955: "It is not Capitalism therefore which is the guardian of Christianity, but Christianity which alone can safeguard free enterprise."[24] These modern-sounding Republican convictions were also evidenced in the Republican affiliation of Henry's late son, the former Michigan Congressman, Paul Henry (1942–1993). The Religious Right's present advocacy of free-market policies in the name of Christian teaching is nothing new. It is just an extension of the old Puritan agenda.

Henry and Graham were by no means solitary Right-leaning voices among the first generation of Evangelical leaders. His successor as editor of *Christianity Today*, Harold Lindsell, regularly articulated defenses of free-market capitalism from enemies on the Left. He even attacked Social Security in 1972, along with critiques of Communism. Such critiques of its materialism were linked to critiques of atheism and relativism.[25] It is also well to keep in mind Bill Bright's efforts in 1976 to mobilize prayer groups for political purposes.[26] The early leaders of the Evangelical Movement clearly sowed the seeds for the formation of the Religious Right.

THE RIGHT TAKES SHAPE

Prior to these developments, with the possible exception of their anti-Catholic voting against Kennedy in 1960, polls indicate that the vast majority of Evangelicals, American Catholics, and several certain mainline Protestant bodies like the American Baptist Churches and certain large segments of American Lutheranism were Democrats.[27] In view of the Puritan-Revivalist ethos of the Movement's leadership this may come as some surprise. However, if we keep in mind how the discrediting of Fundamentalism had relegated the domain of its influence to the rural South and other pockets of less-educated Americans, it is less surprising that so many of these constituents were Democrats. In the South, Democratic support by Evangelicals and Fundamentalists was further undergirded by the heritage of Reconstruction, so that affiliation with the Democratic Party in that region was a means of asserting Southern identity and maintaining segregation.

The openness of some segments of the early Evangelical Movement to Democratic politics is all the more understandable when we keep in mind the bias of non-Puritan traditions, most notably in this case members of Pietist heritages (like Methodists, Holiness Christians, and Pentecostals), along with Catholics and Lutherans, against the free market and in favor of sharing resources. As long as members of these traditions were not incorporated into the Evangelical or Fundamentalist Movement and its pro-capitalist Puritan, modern Revivalist suppositions, openness to Democratic big-government politics did not seem to be in conflict with faith.[28] We will examine that point further in the closing chapters of the book.

However, from the 1940s to the 1970s, membership in Evangelical denominations more than tripled. Correspondingly, the constituency become more middle-class and suburban, than rural and fringe.[29] Economic interests of larger and larger segments of both the Evangelical Movement and even of the Fundamentalist Movement have become a bit more in line with the Republican agenda than in the decades when these constituencies voted Democrat. In this regard, as we shall see, what has happened on the Religious Right is part of a nationwide trend. Another interesting trend is that since 1974 Evangelicals have been more likely to be politically engaged than most Americans.[30]

An additional predecessor to recent trends is evident as early as the 1950s. Evangelicals and Fundamentalists, deeply rooted in Nationalist, Puritan Paradigm sentiments, were among the most vocal of the anti-Communist voices (under the leadership of Billy James Hargis and Carl McIntire) in the McCarthy era (along with criticism of every other segment of the American population not part of the Puritan Paradigm). Another predecessor of recent political trends is evident in much Evangelical literature of the late 1960s through early 1970s, as in face of the legalization of abortion and the Sexual Revolution, numerous publications hit the market concerning divorce, abortion, and homosexuality, along with best sellers on enhancing sex in marriage (such as a 1976 book by Tim and Beverly LaHaye, titled *The Act of Marriage*) and the joys of marital bliss (most successfully marketed by TV personality and former Miss America, Anita Bryant, in her 1971 book, *Amazing Grace*).[31]

The stage was now set for the Religious Right to come to fruition as we know it today. The Carter election in 1976 was the coming-out party. While the mainline denominations had been suffering membership losses since the last part of the 1960s, a 1976 Gallup poll revealed that almost one in five Americans (17 percent), almost one out of every two Protestants, held faith commitments compatible with Evangelical beliefs (defined as having had a born-again experience, holding a literal interpretation of the Bible, and having tried to witness their faith to others).[32] On this basis, along with the election of a self-professed Evangelical to the presidency, *Newsweek* magazine dubbed 1976 "the year of the Evangelical." The spiritual heirs of the once-discredited Fundamentalist Movement were back on the media's map.

To some extent, politicians and their consultants noticed the new importance of this segment of the American population even before the Year of the Evangelical, with the development of the so-called Southern Strategy that got Nixon elected in 1968. But the author of that strategy, Kevin Phillips, articulating the approach in his book *The Emerging Republican Majority*, only tangentially referred to Southern Fundamentalists and Evangelicals in developing the strategy. Of course there was an awareness that "secular liberals" had misjudged the importance of religion in America and that this gave Republicans an important opportunity. But after 1976, this constituency was ready to receive express wooing in the very next Presidential election, which elected Ronald Reagan. In fact, the Southern Baptist Convention's president at that time even expressly articulated his denomination's readiness to contribute to changing America.[33] The year preceding the election was the birthdate of the Moral Majority and, contrary to the usual media version of the lore, its formation was not just a result of the work of the Virginia Baptist Fundamentalist mega-church pastor Jerry Falwell. The development and success of the organization was indeed the beginning of the Religious Right as we know it.

The idea of the Moral Majority was not Falwell's own. He was approached first in 1977 about the idea of forming an organization that would draw on the potential clout of religious television in order to accomplish the political aims of the New Right by a former president of an Evangelical college in Indiana, Robert Billings, who had become a Republican political operative and later served as Ronald Reagan's political liaison to the religious community. (Falwell was already a well-known radio and TV preacher, with his own show, *The Old-Time Gospel Hour*, which had been aired since the time of the founding of his mega-church in Lynchburg, Virginia, in 1956.) A deal was cut two years later when Billings made the same offer, this time along with various New Right Republican strategists.

What is interesting is that what occasioned Billings's and his colleagues' overture and Falwell's engagement was not the famed *Roe v. Wade* decision of the Supreme Court legalizing abortion, but efforts by the IRS to revoke the Evangelical college Bob Jones University's tax-exempt status for the school's racially discriminatory practices.[34] Hardly an auspicious beginning for the Religious Right, and yet its appeal to certain white voters makes even more sense in this light.

The term "Moral Majority" was actually coined by Republican strategist Paul Weyrich, founder of the Heritage Foundation (a think tank for the Right), now head of the Free Congress Foundation, and one of the operatives who sold the idea to Falwell. Another of his ventures has been the American Legislative Exchange Council, which coordinates the work of the Religious Right among state legislatures and advocates giving business a direct hand in writing bills. All these dynamics form the backdrop for the formation of the Moral Majority and the Religious Right as we know it today.[35]

The new organization got off and running with local chapters and plenty of mass communication formats, including direct mailings to Falwell's vast network of religious contacts and a five-day-a-week radio broadcast. Other organizations that formed coalitions with the Moral Majority included the Religious Roundtable, a West Coast organization called Christian Voice, and a "Washington for Jesus" Rally led by Bill Bright and religious TV mogul Pat Robertson. Nearly half a million religious conservatives participated.

The muscle of the new coalition led to some significant successes in the election. Reagan won, as did most of the Republican senatorial candidates whom the Moral Majority supported.[36] These outcomes were further strengthened by the eminent Evangelical author Francis Schaeffer, who advocated forming Christian political organizations to lobby against any government that betrayed Judeo-Christian values. (There are some indications that that he had earlier influenced Falwell.)[37] With such support, it is hardly surprising that in the 1980s, several other influential Right-Wing religious organizations (like the Family Research Council, the Traditional Values Coalition, and Concerned Women for America) were founded, all of which have outlived Falwell's group. The stage was set for Pat Robertson's run for the presidency in 1988, which was refocused in the following year in his formation of the Christian Coalition of America. We will examine these organizations and their profile in the next chapter.

The Moral Majority was not the first of the politically lobbying organizations of the Religious Right (though it exerted the most early impact of the first of these). The Eagle Forum, a conservative women's political organization, was founded in 1972 by Phyllis Schlafly; Focus on the Family was founded in 1977 by James Dobson; and an organization with similar goals, the American Family Association, was founded by Donald Wildmon the same year. Their continuing influence commands our attention in the next chapter.

The Role of the Media in Jesus' Turn to the Right

It is no accident the political operatives who envisaged the Moral Majority approached a radio-TV preacher (who also pastored a mega-church) to be the spokesperson for a conservative version of the Gospel. As the political Right has gained its political clout in part through smart marketing and media savvy, so the Religious Right is intimately connected to the media. Many of its major leaders have links to the media.

We need to be reminded, though, that Jerry Falwell did not invent media ministries. To a large extent the Evangelical Movement, especially in recent years, has dominated this sort of ministry. With this sort of experience, the Religious Right has a longer history of learning how to manipulate the media to its purposes, has more experience learning how to "spin." (Let's get real: Good "spin" is a sine qua non of successful modern politics. To claim to be above it is to resort to a naivete that won't get anyone elected.)

Falwell himself grew up listening to Charles E. Fuller's *Old-Fashioned Revival Hour*, which began in the 1937. Billy Graham's weekly *Hour of Decision* broadcast made its first appearance in 1950. Many of his Crusades have been broadcast on television since that time. Oral

Roberts predates the broadcasts of Falwell, getting his first television program in 1954, and Rex Humbard had his own show for the first time in 1953. The 1960s saw the advent of Jim Bakker's television evangelist career, which ended in scandal and a divorce from his partner Tammy Faye. More significant for our purposes has been Pat Robertson, a Yale Law School lawyer and CEO of his own religious network—the Christian Broadcasting Network, which he began operating in 1961. Control the media, get significant audiences, and you can win not just elections, but also the heart and minds of the public. This is clearly the formula that the Right has used successfully to portray Jesus as a Republican.

The winning formula of the conservative mega-church pastor using the media in order to sell a business-friendly, conservative politic is evident in more recent developments contributing to the coalition between free-market Republicans and theologically conservative Americans. I refer to the emergence of the so-called Prosperity Gospel.

The *Prosperity Gospel* is precisely what the phrase says—the belief that God wants us to prosper, to be rich. Indeed, the more one believes, the more he or she will be loved, and so the more wealth will be gained. The leaders of the movement include televangelists Joyce Meyer (who teaches in her book of the same title that *God's Will Is Prosperity*), Joel Osteen (pastor of the nation's largest congregation, who teaches that God's people deserve and receive "preferential treatment" over everyone else), and, at least prior to his very recent efforts to distance himself somewhat from these positions, T. D. Jakes (an African-American Dallas mega-church pastor who has spoken to the *Dallas Observer* about the "myth of the poor Jesus" which "needs to be destroyed . . . because it holds people back").[38]

Although the Prosperity Gospel leaders are not overtly political like the organizations already covered and to be considered in the next chapter—indeed, two African-American leaders of this movement, Jakes and Atlanta mega-church pastor Eddie Long, do things in and for impoverished communities that would make a liberal Democrat applaud—this strand of recent American church life clearly supports the Religious Right. The morality of these pastors and their congregants is conservative, in line with American Puritan and Revivalist values, and so they become allies for the Right's "moral crusades" against homosexuality and abortion. The connection this sort of preaching posits between spirituality and economic prosperity effectively functions to reinforce the Republican agenda's efforts to maintain its coalition between religious Americans and pro-business interests. If I am an adherent of the Prosperity Gospel, I am more likely to be open to political initiatives that seem to enhance the likelihood of my achieving wealth (cutting taxes, cutting back on social programs for the "unbelieving" poor) or address me in ways that make me think that I am well off (that I will be helped if the inheritance tax is alleviated).

The Prosperity Gospel also did not emerge in a vacuum, but has precedents in American Christianity, several of which we previously pointed out. Televangelist stars of the 1980s like Jimmy Swaggart, Jim and Tammy Bakker, and even earlier Oral Roberts began each show with the promise of increased wealth. We noted how both Billy Sunday and Billy Graham have mixed faith with the promise of material blessings, a combination that at least to some extent is rooted in America's Puritan Paradigm. (We should remind ourselves of the Puritan Cotton Mather's claim that the first generation of Pilgrims "*proceeded* in the evangelical service and worship of our Lord Jesus Christ, so they *prospered* in their secular concernments."[39]) Roberts and, more recently, best-selling author of *The Prayer of Jabez* Bruce Wilkenson teach a "Name It and Claim It" theology that is also in line with Prosperity thinking.[40] With such roots, dating back to the Pilgrim heritage, along with our innate (post-Adamic) selfishness, it is little wonder that Prosperity Gospel and the Republican version of Jesus' faith leading to economic well-being have become so popular. Saturated as we are by the Puritan outlook, the link these preachers posit between faith and prosperity seems so "American."

Another interesting pattern in the success of the Prosperity Gospel suggests insights for understanding both the success of the Religious Right and how to counter its impact. All of these religious leaders associated with the Prosperity Gospel, like their more politically oriented allies on the Right, address large constituencies, both in their churches and/or through their media ministries. The way it works with media exposure (getting interviews and book contracts) is that the larger the audience you address, the more attractive you are to these outlets. But this dynamic entails the likelihood that religious leaders seeking to influence the masses are likely to find business- (i.e., Republican-) friendly postures the most likely to get them hearers and supporters. To debunk the stereotype of Jesus as a conservative is to go against the system's grain.

With this background for the Religious Right, and an awareness of the Puritan-Revivalist ethos of its roots, we can turn in the next chapter to examine the thriving institutions of the movement and to analyze the theological and political convictions that characterize today's Religious Right.

4

The Conservative Jesus

The analysis so far has demonstrated the framework that, with the right kind of publicity and marketing, has led the American public to conclude that Jesus stands for conservative values. The Puritan Paradigm leads religiously inclined Americans (as well as the media unconsciously ensconced in this way of thinking) to regard authentic religion in terms of strict and traditional moral convictions. It also entails that Americans view themselves as an elect nation, one governed by Christian values. Of course, the influence of Revivalism has effectively individualized these social concerns, so that the main sphere of religion in politics for most Americans seems to be at the level of legislating individual morality (abortion, pornography, and homosexuality). In addition, the Puritan Paradigm leads religiously inclined Americans to be quite conservative in their views on Biblical authority and its relation to scientific and historical findings.

The impact of German Enlightenment intellectual suppositions on the leadership of the mainline denominations and society as a whole has apparently not made much of a difference to large segments of the American (Puritan) public. This is evident in twenty-first-century Gallup polls, which reveal that only about one-third of Americans accept Darwin's Theory of Evolution unequivocally, a larger percentage rejecting it outright, while less than half of the population want Evolution taught in the schools. America's Puritan Paradigm presents us with a conservative version of Jesus and the Christian Gospel.

Obviously, then, the organizations and politicians that will matter most to Christians in America are those that tap into this religious conservatism. An examination of the leading organizations of the Religious

Right as well as the political rhetoric of George W. Bush indicates how their impact seems related to their ability to embody these revised Puritan convictions.

THE RELIGIOUS RIGHT

Of course, as we already suggested in the previous chapter, we cannot begin to examine the most significant organizations of the Religious Right today without going back to 1979 and the formation of the Moral Majority. We have noted that although usually only associated with the Fundamentalist preacher Jerry Falwell, the organization was not so much founded by him as by Robert Billings and other Republican operatives.

An examination of the viewpoints of the now largely defunct Moral Majority indicates how many of its key issues seem compatible with America's version of the Puritan Paradigm (and much in line with today's Neo-Conservative agenda). Writing in 1981, Falwell opted for pro-family policies to stem the divorce epidemic, as well as genetic engineering, and, in the name of Jesus Christ, to advocate strong national defense in addition to promoting pro-business policies, along with the reduction of welfare in order to help achieve a sense among African-Americans that they are full citizens.[1] Once again the Puritan commitment to subordinating government policy to Scripture is in evidence, along with the capitalist orientation of that heritage.

Falwell had obviously never been without supporters, even after he dissolved the Moral Majority in 1989. One venture, the recently created *Faith and Values Coalition*, which recruited Falwell protégé Tim LaHaye as board chair, is committed to organizing voters to "vote Christian," advocating for such family values as outlawing gay marriage and abortion.[2]

We have already been reminded of how the Moral Majority was just the beginning of a new round of religiously conservative political activism. Among the still-thriving sister organizations emerging in the years surrounding the Moral Majority's formation is the Traditional Values Coalition founded in 1980 by Reverend Louis Sheldon. Dr. James Dobson formed Focus on the Family in 1977, prior to the Falwell era. We might see the impetus of this organization as more dependent on the dynamics surrounding the election of Jimmy Carter in 1976. However, it should not be overlooked that Dobson himself and subsequently established organizations of the Right became the major political players that they are (Dobson became a Presidential advisor in the Reagan years and a Senate majority advisor during the 1990s) only after the Moral Majority had its greatest impact in electing Reagan. It helps to remind us that the Religious Right as a whole, and even the significance of Dobson's work, has been largely indebted to the rise of Falwell's organization.

In the last chapter we also pointed out the significance of the 1988 Presidential campaign of the Reverend Pat Robertson for the present impact and growth of the political organizations of the Religious Right. The primary outcome of that campaign was the formation of the Christian Coalition of America, founded a year after his unsuccessful run. The organization has had its ups and downs since its establishment (ups occurred especially during the leadership of Ralph Reed, as it played an instrumental role in getting out the vote in 1994 when the Republicans took over the Senate and the House). It even explored building coalitions with politically and ethically conservative Catholics, although such outreach has been more or less abandoned recently as the coalition has fallen on harder times, even being abandoned by several of its local state chapters. However, although he is not officially part of the Coalition's leadership, it continues to be supported by Robertson's *700 Club*, still broadcast on the Family Entertainment Network to which Robertson sold his Christian Broadcasting Network. As a result, and because of its continuing membership, the Christian Coalition of America continues at press time to be a force with which to reckon, especially for Republican candidates.

The Religious Right and its influential political lobbying organizations have not only become a political force. They have also effectively defined Christianity and Christian social ethics for the media—and through those means, for the American public. Institutionally, this is how Jesus and Christianity have become conservative and Republican. We will now examine the underlying suppositions of the major political organizations of the Religious Right. This will demonstrate why their version of Christianity, trading on suppositions of the Puritan Paradigm, has been so widely influential.

Today's Powerhouse Organizations

Some of the organizations formed in the wake of the Moral Majority have become significant political players for the theologically conservative segments of American Christianity. We have already noted a number of them: Pat Robertson's Christian Coalition of America (for a time steered so successfully by its former Executive Director Ralph Reed); James Dobson's *Focus on the Family*; Donald Wildmon's *American Family Association*; and the *Traditional Values Coalition*. Affiliated with the Robertson organization has been the American Center for Law and Justice, the legal arm of the Christian Coalition intended to function as the Right's version of the ACLU. Its policy aims have been to legally advocate for bans on abortion and gay civil unions.

The *Traditional Values Coalition*, founded in 1980 by Louis Sheldon, has an especially active and capable lobbying program critical of legislation related to gay rights, abortion, and the teaching of Evolution in schools. In this regard it shares the agenda of Dobson's very influential and powerful *Focus on the Family* founded in 1977, though the latter also purchases television time reaching a broad audience (25.6 million every week in America) and has an educational agenda, including support for school prayer and educational vouchers.[3] Other organizations devoted to these "family values" issues have been formed. These include the *Family Research Council*, also founded by Dobson as a think-tank and lobby for the issues of Focus on the Family. It is one of a number of family action or family policy councils, most of which are legally independent, but affiliated with Focus on the Family. Since 1988 this organization has been led by a real political heavyweight, Gary Bauer, Reagan's chief domestic policy advisor. Another member of this lobbying organization's leadership, Tony Perkins, has an unfortunate record of engagement with white supremacist organizations.[4] Also noteworthy is the *Arlington Group*, founded in 2003, which represents seventy national Fundamentalist organizations to defeat the "homosexual agenda." In any case, given this sort of lobbying expertise and national media, one can better appreciate the influence of Dobson's policies in our present political context.

Two other influential organizations have similar agendas, though their focus has been to curtail the influence of the Feminist Movement. The newer one was organized by Tim LaHaye's wife Beverly in 1979,

Concerned Women for America. The older organization, the *Eagle Forum*, was founded in 1972 by the eminent critic of Feminism, Phyllis Schlafly (b. 1924). Originally established to lobby against the proposed Feminist-inspired Equal Rights Amendment, the organization came to take on the broader agenda of opposing gay rights, federal support for daycare, and U.S. membership in the United Nations, as well as lobbying for public school curricular reform, which would ensure curricula that would not violate "Christian values." The Puritan-like agenda of a society governed by Christian principles is again apparent in this agenda. Schlafly's notoriety and media contacts made the Eagle Forum, along with the Family Research Council and the Christian Coalition, one of the most influential Christian Right advocacy groups.[5]

We need to consider a less well-known, but profoundly influential organization founded by Tim LaHaye, the famed mega-church pastor and best-selling author, and wealthy businessman Joseph Coors in 1981, the *Council for National Policy*. It is an umbrella organization to make possible networking among leaders of the most important conservative political groups, conservative politicians, and some of America's wealthiest family dynasties. *ABC News* is reported to have identified the Council as "the most powerful conservative group you've never heard of" and the *New York Times* called it "the club of the most powerful . . . , the genuine leaders of the Republican Party."[6]

Kevin Phillips overstates the case that this organization has been co-opted, like the Religious Right as a whole, by a fringe theological movement called Christian Reconstructionism, which calls for the practice and advocacy of a theocracy. Of course, the Puritan strands of various members of the Religious Right find affinity with this movement, and it is true that several members of the Council for National Policy may be Reconstructionists. But their number is so small as not to warrant the conclusion that the Religious Right is fundamentally in the sway of Reconstructionist thinking.[7]

Another highly influential organization, but barely known by the public is a small group of wealthy Evangelicals called *Legacy*. Founded by two Dallas businessmen, Ray Washburn and George Seay, it is functioning to screen Republican candidates in order to determine which ones receive support.

The *Southern Baptist Convention* is also now a major political player in Washington, through its lobby headed by Richard Land. The conservative swing of the Convention accomplished in 1979 is also to some extent a child of the era of the Carter Presidency's making Evangelical Christianity credible again, as well as Falwell's notoriety.

The Right's (Puritan) Version of Jesus Christ and His Gospel

We can see in the impact of each of these organizations an ability to address issues that reflect the agenda of the revised American version of the Puritan Paradigm. With their conservative theological orientation, all of these organizations are able to address Puritanism's and the American public's appreciation of the authority of the Bible. The most recent May 2006 Gallup poll on the subject found that 77 percent of Americans viewed the Bible as in some sense divinely inspired, an indication that the conservative beliefs of the Puritans about the Bible are still having an impact on the American public.

We have also noted that many of these organizations share the American Revivalist heritage's concern with personal morality. Consider the preoccupation with speaking out and lobbying against choice on abortion, homosexuality, and protected-sex sex education in the schools by Focus on the Family, the American Family Association, Eagle Forum, and the Traditional Values Coalition.

Much in the tradition of later nineteenth-century Revivalism and American Revivalist traditions since that time, the focus of Christian attention is not on structural questions about how to end poverty, racism, and other forms of injustice, but instead concerns itself with personal morality (as interpreted through a literal, noncritical reading of the Bible) (Mark 10:7–9; Psalm 139:13; Luke 1:44; Romans 1:26–27). Note here the Biblical literalism of these organizations.

All of these organizations, as well as the Christian Coalition and the Southern Baptist lobby, are seeking to bring what they consider to be "Christian values" to bear on the public square. This commitment is part of the SBC Articles of Faith, affirmed in Article XV of its *Baptist Faith and Message*. It manifests itself in the case of the Christian Coalition; founder Pat Robertson has not only advocated vouchers to permit parents to enroll children in private church schools, but also to have Christian principles taught in public schools. In fact, he has even gone so far as to critique the separation of church and state (at least as it is presently interpreted by the judicial branch) and even to refer to America as "founded as a Christian nation." Similar views have been articulated by another prominent televangelist and proponent of the Religious Right, Dr. James Kennedy.[8]

As we have noted, this subordination of the state to Christian values is precisely what the early Puritans, even those in the tradition of the Mayflower Pilgrims, aimed to do. The First Amendment notwithstanding, large numbers of the American public (especially churchgoing Protestant Christians) have embodied this Puritan way of thinking, viewing America as a "Christian nation."

Relatively recent poll data bear out the enduring character of these Puritan convictions. According to a Pew Forum poll held just prior to the 2004 election, over one-half of the public would have reservations voting for a candidate with no religious affiliation (31 percent refusing to vote for a Muslim and 15 percent for a Catholic). Pat Robertson himself has expressed such thinking.[9] In a similar July 2005 poll, over half the public would have churches express their political views. In view of the poll data, it is little wonder that these organizations of the Right, which militantly advocate what significant numbers of the electorate believe (the fact that these organizations are not churches also helps their stature when they offer political judgments), would pack so much political clout.

A number of these organizations, most notably the Christian Coalition, the Council for National Policy, and to a lesser extent and not as officially, the Southern Baptist Convention and Focus on the Family, have more expressly defined their mission in terms of aiming to control the agenda of the Republican Party.[10] In establishing these links with the party of American business, men like the SBC's Richard Land, Pat Robertson, and Tim LaHaye are doing nothing at odds with the beliefs of the first Puritans of seventeenth-century England and their small-government, pro-capitalist agenda. The espousal of this agenda is made all the more credible in some Christian circles by the fact that many Americans are at least implicitly hearing the free market extolled on Sundays through Prosperity Gospel preaching. A Revivalist-influenced version of Puritanism will find coalitions with politically conservative organizations like these natural alliances. The result of the fusion of all these forces and dynamics is a conservative version of Jesus and His Gospel.

But, of course, even at the top of government we find this sort of Jesus. And that version of the Messiah gets even more free press than the organizations we have examined. Let's then take a brief look at George W. Bush's Jesus.

THE PRESIDENTIAL JESUS:
GEORGE BUSH'S VERSION OF THE GOSPEL

David Aikman has written a whole volume on this subject. But he misses the correlation between the President's faith and the Puritan Paradigm of American religion.[11] Thus, just a brief summary is appropriate.

In some respects George Bush's religious rhetoric has been no more pronounced than that of most recent American Presidents, including Jimmy Carter. In fact, there are some in Bush's corner who are likely to argue that their President is simply embodying the religious viewpoint embedded in American founding documents.[12] Let's consider some relevant theological reflections by George Bush.

In an August 13, 2002, radio address to the nation, the President referred to those who oppose us as "evil." This seems to be a recurring theme in his rhetoric since 9/11. Indeed, he has spoken of ridding the world of evil.[13]

Correspondingly, Bush rhetoric has included claims, such as in his 2003 State of the Union address, that "there's power, wonder-working power in the goodness and idealism and faith of the American people." The President also relates freedom closely to the will of God. As he put it in his 2004 State of the Union address: "I believe that God has planted in every heart the desire to live in freedom. . . . So America is pursuing a forward strategy of freedom in the Middle East." President Bush seems very certain that God and good are on the American side.

Speaking at Ellis Island in 2002 on the first anniversary of the 9/11 attacks, the President echoed these sentiments and the American Puritan belief in the chosenness of Americans. He claimed, "this ideal of America is the hope of all mankind." Such an equation of Christianity with nationalism has deep resonance in the American psyche as a result of our Puritan spiritual roots and its stress on covenant and election.[14]

Early Puritans in England and their American heirs may not have agreed with the President that people (Americans) can be without evil. But as we have seen, such optimism typifies much later nineteenth- and twentieth-century Revivalism. At the very least, the confidence Bush has in the American electorate for a divine task, where others are evil but Americans aren't, has clear parallels to Puritan beliefs regarding the confidence that those elected by God experience concerning their election. He even reportedly understands his Presidency as a consequence of God's will.[15]

Despite his Methodism, the President's belief that God is involved in the world's affairs clearly bespeaks a Puritan orientation.[16] At the 2003 National Prayer Breakfast he claimed that "behind all of life and all of history, there's a dedication and purpose, set by the hand of a just and faithful God." Some interpreters argue that this is simply what the Declaration of Independence teaches, which in its last paragraph refers to "reliance on the protection of divine Providence." What may be different, though, is the impersonal character of the Declaration's reference to deity, a reference that entails that its god may not in fact be directly involved in our lives as Bush's Christian vision obviously understands God to be. In this regard, his nearest ally is obviously Puritanism, which opted for a sovereign, very "hands-on" God with regard to managing the world's affairs.

It is true that George Bush sometimes seems to appeal to the natural law. For example, he claimed at the 2001 National Prayer Breakfast that "Men and women can be compassionate without faith, but faith often inspires compassion." (The idea that compassion is in principle known by all and is an expectation of all clearly embodies a natural-law perspective.) In the same spirit, Bush also has claimed that Muslims worship the same God as Christians do. Along similar lines has been his rejection of homosexuality on grounds of how fundamental marriage is to society, not by express appeal to the Will of God. (Of course, to some extent Puritans also embraced these commitments, affirming the concept of the natural law and the idea that everything the Ten Commandments teach is accessible to all people.[17]) Also note how Bush does not make it clear that he believes non-Christians can see the validity of his other national and international initiatives as Christians can.

At other points, though, the President and his supporters have opted for much more distinctively Christian—even Puritan—arguments for their policies. The faith-based initiative proposals, using faith-based institutions to deliver social welfare programs, are certainly a good cost-cutting measure, a chance to cut big government. But it also puts the Church and society in the sort of tandem relationship that characterizes Puritanism.[18]

Other examples of Republican rhetoric endorsing Puritan commitments should be noted. I have already called attention to Bush's rhetoric regarding the War on Terror. In speaking of it as a "war against evil," he added in his 2002 State of the Union address that it is also a (religious) "crusade to defend freedom."

We have already noted how the President relates freedom to the Will of God. This point, coupled with his language about the war in Iraq as a "crusade," seem to suggest that God is always on the side of freedom and those who defend it, so that to fight for freedom is a Christian task. Of course the President has seemed to balance this with comments suggesting that freedom is something that all people have access to apart from faith, as when he claimed in a 2003 speech for the National Endowment for Democracy that "liberty is the design of nature." He also says, though, that it is "the plan of Heaven," a comment that brings it back to a theistic context and removes his ethical norms merely from the realm of the natural law. Again it is evident that in fighting this war, Americans in the Republican worldview are doing God's business, fighting a kind of holy war. At this point too, we see something like the Puritan subordination of political affairs to Christian norms and the Will of God at work.

At many other points Bush's domestic policy agenda resonates with the Puritan vision, especially in seeming to subordinate the state to Christian values. Although he has not heretofore invoked the Will of God or distinct Christian teachings to authorize efforts to promote marriage or promote religion-based alternatives to the Theory of Evolution in American schools, these positions have enough resonance with his religiously conservative allies ensconced in the Puritan mind-set to be heard as efforts to promote Christian values in American society.

Of course the overall Bush agenda also resonates with America's Puritan ethos. His personal commitment to small government (at least as he articulates it), the promotion of business interests, and the de-emphasis on the plight of the poor, all advanced by a Christian man presumably influenced by the Gospel's teachings, also lend an air of Puritan worldview to his Presidency. And as we have seen, the more Puritan (post-Revivalism, with a God Who does not interfere with our freedom) you are, the more American Christians are likely to see you as on their side. And Bush's espousal of Intelligent Design Theory and its critique of Evolution further reinforces in the public a sense that he shares its conservative views about

Scripture. When you can embody Puritan ways of thinking and your opponent does not, you not only seem more religious, you seem more American to many religious Americans. Until 2006, this was the formula for the conservative Republican hegemony. Polls indicate that it still works very effectively with Christian voters.

SOLIDIFYING JESUS' CONSERVATISM

The power of the media, along with a Democratic Party elite more concerned with socially liberal white-collar professionals who largely do not go to church, has effectively led the American public to interpret the President's and Right's conservative policies as the only legitimate Christian alternatives. This chapter has been about how by trading on the Revivalist-amended American Puritan Paradigm the Religious Right has succeeded in seducing the constituencies of once-Democratic strongholds like the Southern Baptist Convention, the Roman Catholic Church, and even of Midwestern Lutheranism and segments of the African-American Church (witness the support of conservatism provided by mega-church black pastors like Bishop Eddie Long), as well as bodies previously open to big-government economic policies like the American Baptist Churches and The United Methodist Church. Inasmuch as since Colonial times Puritanism has been deemed, at least subliminally, to be the most American way to be religious, and since it opts for a conservative personal ethic characterized by duty, a conservative theological posture on Biblical authority, a pro-capitalist, small-government ethos (especially as modified by the individualism of Revivalism), and a subordination of the state to Christian values, (at least as the ideal), it is little wonder that the agendas of the Democratic Party and the intellectual leadership of the mainline denominations would be deemed secular or non-Christian. After all, these people opt for big-government programs for the poor, are socially liberal, and if they do believe, they opt for critical readings of the Bible and relativism. Those people don't seem Christian according to the dominant American way of doing Christianity. That's how Jesus and His Gospel have gotten conservative and Republican.

To turn these attitudes around would demand that spokespersons for American religion, particularly Christians in the numerically dominant mainline Protestant, African-American, and Catholic churches help the public to see that the Right's version of Jesus is not the only way, maybe not even the correct one. This entails that in order to turn things around, the theologians and professors of American religion need to communicate this alternative vision of Jesus to the politicians and the public in general. If they fail, the laity in the more "liberal" churches would need to draw on the heritage of their churches to withstand the Religious Right's Puritan-Revivalist construal of faith. It sounds like a winner. But on a widespread, politically significant level it has not been happening. And given present trends, I don't think it's likely to happen too soon. The cutting-edge theology and the teaching of these churches has been caught up in modernist, post-Enlightenment suppositions to such an extent that these theologies and the students who are taught them have no tools to criticize the Republican version of the faith. Also, the proponents of these modern theologies are so far removed from American Puritan-Revivalist thought as to not even be capable of communicating with people in the pews or of criticizing the dominant paradigm. The result is that the average member of these churches (even the regular churchgoers) no longer learns the faith from his or her church. As generations pass, the traditional denominational or cultural faith that was taught sometimes in a counter-cultural way in these churches has been lost. All that is left to learn under these circumstances is the civil religion that still circulates even in secularized American society, the Puritan Paradigm's version of faith (modified by Revivalism). Such a constituency is ready to hear the Republican version of the faith and its associated politics as the only Christian option.[19] Let's take a look in the next chapters at exactly how these trends cashed out. These insights may teach these churches, the Democrats, and their friends some lessons about what it will take to communicate a fresh message about religion and justice.

II

WHY IT'S UNLIKELY TO GET BETTER SOON

5

American Theological Education since World War II

One of the reasons for the present dominance of the conservative Republicans' version of Jesus has been the impotence of mainline theology since World War II. American theological education finally "caught up" with Europe. But given the present quality of Western European church life, being able to do theology like and with the British, Germans, French, Dutch, or Scandinavians is no guarantee of effectiveness.

The fact that American theological education (as well as the university system) has in some sense caught up with Western Europe is quite an accomplishment. Until after World War II, no one in Europe paid any attention to American theologians (except for immigrants to America like the famous Existentialist Theologian Paul Tillich [1886–1965]). In virtually every denomination, except perhaps Baptist and Methodist/ Holiness schools (which were quite few), professors directed their students to books by scholars from Western Europe. That is no longer the case today, as a result of the realization of trends set off in the 1950s and 1960s. What has happened to make this possible to some extent is that American theological education, like the university system in general, has "transcended" its uniquely American ways in favor of adopting the suppositions that have dominated Western European life and churches since the Enlightenment.

Even the methods of instruction that came to be adopted—the lecture, and eventually some seminars—were borrowed from the Western European system of education, taking the place of the older style based on memorization and recitation by students coupled with mentoring their spiritual lives. The first of these new methods afforded more opportunities for the development of manuscripts that could be transformed into articles and books.

We might put it this way: America might have conquered the Germans, but the Germans won the war over the ethos of the American academy.[1] The more American theology came to resemble the modes of Western Europe, the more it came to receive global respect. (Recall that in the middle of the twentieth century, everywhere else in the world Protestant and Catholic churches were looking to Western Europe for inspiration and accreditation for their intellectual lives.)

Of course, it is not the case that American theology was totally devoid of contact and dialogue with the suppositions of the European Enlightenment prior to World War II. We all know of the Enlightenment's impact on America's Founders in the eighteenth century. But it was not the English, Scottish, and French Enlightenment figures who influenced them, like the nineteenth-century German scholars who began to influence American theology after the 1940s. It is also significant to recall that the Founders were America's elite, and so their ideas did not filter down to the masses for generations.

It is also true that some American theologians and seminaries were in dialogue with German Enlightenment ideas as early as the latter part of the nineteenth century. The Fundamentalist Movement was a reaction against the teaching of these views in Ivy League schools and the endorsement of them by significant numbers of alumni of these institutions. But until the decades after World War II this was not widespread. Only at the elite seminaries (like those of the Ivy League or the Rockefeller-funded University of Chicago) were the ideas of philosophers Immanuel Kant (1724–1804) and G. W. F. Hegel (1770–1831), psychologist Sigmund Freud (1856–1939), sociologist Max Weber (1864–1920), Darwin's Theory of Evolution, and the method of historical criticism of Biblical literature taught. These schools were also teaching a mediating approach to theology rooted in German soil called Neo-Orthodoxy, which sought to mediate Enlightenment worldviews and a more traditional literalistic view of Biblical authority. It would take until the 1950s (and in some cases the 1960s) for these ideas to become widely and sympathetically accepted in virtually every mainline denominational seminary. As the 1960s waned, Neo-Orthodoxy was fading away to be replaced by the approaches described in this chapter. (Of course, these trends did not make headway in Fundamentalist and Evangelical seminaries, except to receive words of criticism from faculty.)

Another way in which American theological education looked better to Europeans after World War II was a function of more pastors receiving a seminary education beginning in the 1950s. Prior to that era, pastors from Methodist and Baptist mainline denominations were not mandated to earn a seminary (or even a college) degree. But beginning in the 1950s with the "professionalization" of the ministry (the idea that pastors were professionals, like other "credentialed" professionals such as teachers, lawyers, and doctors), even these denominations gradually began to require a seminary degree of candidates for the ministry.

In lots of ways, the new trends seemed to be good for the American Church. However, the new educational ethos has led to a breaking with American ways in favor of a kind of a Bohemian spirit with little use for the bourgeoisie. In the last four decades, such attitudes in the theological academy have effectively alienated mainline seminaries and their theologies from the people in the pews.[2] Correspondingly, church leaders trained in this ethos have likewise largely become alienated from the American mainstream. More on that in the next chapter. For the present, it is enough to say that the alienation of American mainline academic theology has effectively muzzled the mainline denominations' ability to critique the Republican version of a conservative Jesus.

As we shall note, the adoption of these German Enlightenment suppositions tends to turn the faithful "inward," to focus on their own personal well-being and in turn to orient themselves away from the social concerns that the conservative version of Jesus also ignores. As a result, this new theological orientation results in both the Left and the Right neglecting the poor and questions of economic justice. Even for those theologians who would present an alternative vision of Jesus and religion, with a God Who cares for the poor and recognizes the need to create structures that safeguard minorities, they do not have categories to communicate this message convincingly to what remains of the Puritan-Revivalist piety of the American public. Let's take a look at these dynamics in more detail.

HOW THE NEW MODELS OF AMERICAN THEOLOGY FAIL TO COMMUNICATE AN ALTERNATIVE

The view of reality mid-twentieth century Americans had inherited from the Founders, like Europeans prior to the Enlightenment and most other premodern people, was to believe that we can reason together. Some things are just common sense. Of course the idea of "common sense" was embedded in the popular American psyche by the famous pro-Revolutionary pamphlets of Thomas Paine (1737–1809) titled *Common Sense*. A number of the Founders, notably John Witherspoon, the only clergyman to sign the Declaration of Independence, his student James Madison, and one of the most influential undergraduate instructors of Thomas Jefferson were influenced by a philosophical school of the Scottish Enlightenment called Common Sense Realism.[3] Among its core suppositions was that, just as some things are common sense, so we can objectively receive truth and can achieve a "common meaning" of things.[4]

Even if we concede that some of the Founders were not so clearly influenced by the Common Sense Realists, but by the eminent British proponent of empiricism, John Locke (1632–1704), the case can be made for their endorsement of the objectivity of knowledge. This was clearly Locke's own position.[5] And we should not overlook the Declaration of Independence's appeal to "self-evident" truths.

In the nineteenth and early twentieth century the American public continued to speak of common sense and believed in the possibility of objective truth. Even significant segments of the African-American community of the nineteenth century appealed to common sense in the Constitution as their framework for ending slavery.[6]

All was well with American common sense until the advent of Immanuel Kant on the American scene. Although he had had great impact on the European Continent for decades, effectively becoming *the* philosopher for modern Protestant theology, his widespread impact on the American academy and theological education effectively became widespread only since the end of World War II.

Kant's philosophy is a challenge to the belief in the possibility of objective truth. He posited distinction between the noumenon (the thing in itself) and the phenomenon (one's perception of the noumenal reality).[7] Essentially, this scheme critiques the idea of common sense, since it entails that all knowledge is relative to the individual's perception of it. Given Kantian suppositions, we can never achieve knowledge in itself, objective knowledge, and truth. Such relativism has slowly made headway in becoming acceptable to Americans, but it did not happen overnight. As recently as 1991, according to a Barna Research Group poll, strong believers in the possibility of attaining absolute truth still outnumbered those strongly insisting that truth can be described in radically distinct ways.[8] It is evident that resistance to Kantian insights would even have been stronger in earlier years. To embrace Kantian suppositions was, until recently, to go against the grain of American popular opinion.

What has happened in almost all mainline denominations since the 1950s has been the propagation of this sort of perspectival thinking, and it has impacted the theology taught in their seminaries. This is not surprising because cutting-edge Western European Theology has opted for this relativism since the nineteenth century. It is evident in the theology of the famed nineteenth-century German theologian Friedrich Schleiermacher (1768–1834), who is generally recognized as the father of modern Christian theology (and so functions as the paradigm for most postwar mainline American theology).[9]

Essentially, Schleiermacher was responding to new insights about history and science that seemed to challenge the veracity of the literal common sense meaning to the Biblical texts and classical Christian doctrines. The Theory of Evolution and other modern scientific/genetic theories are widely presupposed in most American institutions of higher learning. Likewise, most of these schools embrace critical readings of the Bible (which challenge Moses' authorship of the first five Books, Paul's authorship of several Epistles traditionally ascribed to him, and make critical theories about a "Q" [an ancient compilation of Jesus' authentic sayings], which is said to form the basis for the Gospels, which were written decades later). It is evident, then, that Schleiermacher's issues in his context have been challenges to the faith that American candidates for the ministry have needed to address since the 1950s, if not before.

The great modern German theologian's method in response to these challenges was to bypass the literal, objective meaning of these texts and concepts in favor of reading them allegorically in order to identify their "depth" meaning—their message hidden under the literal verbiage. In order to get to this deeper meaning he correlated the Word of God in the Biblical text and these doctrines with an intellectually acceptable set of concepts that provides the language into which the deeper truth of the Word is to be translated.[10] This sort of Method-of-Correlation approach or an equivalent largely dominates the thinking of most professors in mainline seminaries. Note its presupposition—that the language used to describe the truth (God's Word) is not essential. Consequently, the same truth contained in both Scripture and the Tradition can be expressed in different forms. In other words, there is no one way to express truth, no one truth. It is all a matter of the perspective you bring to God's Word. The Kantian suppositions are obvious. We can never get the Truth (to the Word of God) in itself.[11]

This reliance on Kant is not just characteristic of Schleiermacher. It is embedded in the thinking of every theologian who relies on the Method of Correlation. In short, the relativism that characterizes Kant's thinking is in the background of the prevailing models of contemporary theology taught in the mainline American seminaries. This is not just a Protestant hang-up; two of the most prominent Roman Catholic theologians of the postwar era and their disciples embrace this idea that all we know about God and the world is relative to our experience of it.[12] At least to some extent, then, this sort of relativistic version of Christian faith is being propounded in mainline congregations.

The implicit espousal of this relativistic outlook in the mainline denominations not only has negative implications for the spirituality they nurture. In pointing out the dominance of these philosophical suppositions and the associated theological model of mainline American denominations, identifying these developments as being responsible for much of the problems these churches face, I have a great deal in common with analysis of mainline Protestant decline offered by the eminent Evangelical sociologist Tony Campola. But he does not go into enough detail regarding precisely how such relativism fails these denominations. I will show that it is not just the failure of this academic model to address experiential issues or a bureaucratization of church life or the taking of social positions out of touch with the membership, that accounts for mainline decline.[13] But that is a topic for another book someday.

At any rate, I also want to highlight how the relativistic model these denominations espouse at the highest levels of church life is politically problematic in our present context. Given these suppositions, whenever one of the mainline denominations' leaders or these denominations themselves take positions contrary to the Right's (such as pro-life, pro-gay, pro-civil rights positions), as several of them affirm, the grounds for these positions appear to be relativistic.[14] On methodological grounds that characterize the theological ethos of these denominations,

Scripture and Tradition are not literally invoked. And so the way in which the heritage is mined boils down to a matter of the interpreter's (subjective) starting point for interpretation. And since the Right contends by contrast to have the literal (objective) sense of Scripture on their side, it can market the authority and truth of its conclusions, while liberal Catholics and the mainline Protestant churches can do little more than make a vague appeal to their sense of justice and values. In the marketplace of ideas, the Right's conservative version of Jesus has a better "spin."

The dynamics I have been describing in the American theological academy are just the tip of the iceberg, pertaining to the first wave of post-World War II American theology. But since the 1970s, if not before, additional dynamics deriving from Kantian relativism have rendered theological education in the mainline denominations even more problematic.

DeConstruction, Nihilism, and the Therapeutic Ethos: Relativism Runs Wild in the Academy

The Kantian relativistic vision has fostered the development of the social sciences, and that has had significant impact on American (and European) theological scholarship. The widespread introduction of the father of sociology Max Weber into the curriculum of cutting-edge universities, and eventually into the theological jargon of seminaries, has further cemented relativistic thinking among educated Americans. His insight about our need for values, though they cannot be sustained in light of some grand theodicy (speculation about God's purposes in the world) since all of them depend on human creativity and are shaped by social circumstances, has been received in America (contrary to Weber's own tragic outlook on the state of things) with a naive optimism that gives us permission "to do our thing."[15]

If values are something you make up as you go along, the door is opened to Nihilism. Little wonder, then, after the introduction of Weber into the American academy that the German Enlightenment's most (in)famous Nihilist, Friedrich Nietzsche became the celebrity he was in the American academy through much of the 1960s and 1970s (if not still today). If we do not need his daring call to create our own values, lest the establishment impose its agenda on us so much today, it is because most Americans who hang around universities and seminaries, along with our media stars and gurus, already "know" it. Besides, as we will see, the new academic infatuation with DeConstruction is really Nietzschean. These views are all over the mainline academic theology today, if not in American society as a whole; we commonly refer to the valuing of all religion equally, to the difference between white men's and African-American readings of texts, to different readings by different genders, to "lifestyles," "commitment," and "identity."[16] The popular word "multiculturalism" has come to be interpreted in this way.

Into this gap, a sanitized (more optimistic) version of Sigmund Freud and his therapeutic insights arrives. Convinced that there is nothing to values but the self, Americans became self-preoccupied, single-minded about caring for the self, its feelings, and the self's fulfillment.[17] Psychiatry and its stepsister, psychology, become the new religion for modern Americans, the new way to happiness and meaning. Consider the popularity (if not at present, at least in the most recent decades) of phrases like "getting in touch with your feelings," "having your needs met," "self-esteem," "dysfunctional," and "being good to yourself," and you begin to get a flavor for how thoroughly saturated Americans are with a therapeutic mind-set.

With the 1950s and the push for professionalizing white-collar jobs, along with the increased lack of confidence in the objective truth of religion in mainline Protestantism and (later in the next decade) Catholicism, theological education began to see the categories of the new religion (psychology) as an apt intellectually credible way of explaining and evaluating what clergy do. That is just what has happened, as now clergy of these traditions are evaluated for ordination in terms of psychological fitness and taught to minister and think about the faith in these categories. Church is more about helping people find peace of mind and happiness than about praising God and nurturing lives of self-sacrificial service (agape love).[18]

Other intellectual characteristics emerge from this conglomeration of convictions, all of them with significant impact today on mainline theology and the way its students are educated. Since guilt is to be overcome by therapy, theology needed to rethink its view of sin and guilt. A whole rethinking of these concepts has followed, and it has largely won the day in the elite segments of the academy as well as in the mainline pews. Establishing healthy self-esteem is now deemed *the* task of ministry. Tied up with this perspective has been a sense that ethics (the rules of right and wrong, understood objectively as God's Commandments) impinge on our freedom.[19] This fits with the therapeutic ethos, which teaches nonjudgmental habits of minds. Tolerance fits here, as the essence of sociability, undergirding the academy's commitment to multiculturalism. But given these suppositions, is anything ever wrong? Typically the problem gets handled by critically appropriating the Commandments in such a way that you are not universally condemned, but are deemed capable of fulfilling the Commands now that they are interpreted in the modern mode you have selected. Love your neighbor now means love yourself.[20]

Into this mix, the academy in the last two or three decades has spoken of our being in a *Post-Modern Era* and found an ally in a literary-analytic approach called DeConstruction. Of course it is not clear how the modern era has been transcended, for proponents of this view are just as ensconced in Kantian suppositions as anytime in the academy since World War II. Perhaps what is "post-modern" is that now these assumptions and the relativism associated with them have filtered down to the masses, whereas previously American encounters with the Enlightenment had included a robust belief that objective truth was possible to achieve, a matter of common sense.

In a society where everyone knows that truth is relative to the subject, we need to "deconstruct" accepted meanings of texts and social circumstances if we are to be true to ourselves. Most in the academy have come to recognize, with the DeConstructionist scholars, that ultimately the works canonized as classics and standard interpretations are constructions created in the interests of preserving the social power of the elites.[21] With these suppositions, it seems we can no longer confess the faith together, and besides, it is your own creative appropriation of the faith that matters.

It is why each ethnic group and gender needs its own theology. This is the way Biblical studies, Church history, and even Systematic Theology are conducted in most mainline seminaries today.

As I previously suggested, this set of assumptions leads its adherents to a bohemian attitude with regard to American ways of life. There is a generally critical attitude toward American ways in the mainline seminaries' theological ethos, hardly surprising given the non-American suppositions with which theology is now conducted on these campuses.

This anti-American viewpoint surfaced in the 1960s with regular condemnations of American foreign policy, blaming the United States for the arms race and Vietnam. Since that time it has surfaced again in these seminaries' support of Liberation Theology, which characteristically includes a developing-world critique of American global hegemony; Liberation Theology is also associated with Feminist Theology and gay ordination, which critique most of the core institutions of American society for their homophobic, patriarchal orientation. Even the academy's preoccupation with multiculturalism and diversity typically includes critique of American values and institutions, in favor of a pluralism that finds little favorable in both America's Constitutional and economic systems. The Puritan Paradigm's endorsement of America as a "chosen people" is under assault.

There is no way such a theology can have much impact on the American social psyche, save to reinforce the media and business establishment's narcissistic individualism. In fact, its suppositions court rejection by the segments of the public still formed by traditional suppositions. So as long as the more liberal version of Jesus of mainline Protestant and Catholic churches is couched in this sort of theology, do not expect much success—much prophetic impact on American public life. Of course, this style of theology has had significant impact on the mainline churches and its seminaries. As we shall see, it is unwittingly either assisting in nurturing pieties that will embrace ("consume") the business interests of Republicans or it is encouraging a backlash that leads the disgruntled to embrace conservative Evangelicalism and its Republican political agenda.

6

Impact of German Philosophy and Theology on the Pews: The Impotence of Today's Cutting-Edge Theologies

The trends in mainline American theological education have reached the pews, but not to the good of the Church or to the good of liberal politics. Although American Christianity as a whole is far from theologically literate, a combination of preaching in the congregation along with the media's marketing of the Enlightenment suppositions we have been examining have created enough awareness of these trends to be imbibed and even endorsed in the mainline Protestant and even Catholic pews. Such an awareness has led others in the same congregations (and in Evangelical and Fundamentalist pews) to conclude that they must reject such "secular humanism." Examples are legion. The cumulative effect of all the examples we will examine is that they have effectively rendered the mainline denominations impotent to address prophetically the important issues of the day. Of course they say that they are "prophetic," insofar as the leadership of these denominations often hold some convictions in tension with the American grassroots. But in fact, even on most of these occasions, the mainline denominations, largely due to the dynamics sketched in the last chapter, are merely following the trends of media gurus and the cultural elite, to the benefit of Republican interests.

The previous chapter captured the ethos of academia today, largely marked by a kind of bohemian relativism and attuned to therapeutic agendas of self-respect and self-fulfillment. After three post–World War II generations who went to college in larger percentages than any previous generations in American history, these attitudes in the academic ethos, along with their permeation of media culture have filtered down into American society as a whole, even into the largest and oldest mainline denominations.

Many examples can be cited. The growing Biblical illiteracy in these churches is one notable correlate of the way theological education is now widely conducted, with an emphasis on criticizing the Bible and our inability to discern what it really means. Recent Gallup polls indicate a clear decline in American society as a whole with regard to how many believe the Bible is literally the true Word of God. A more recent (2005) Barna Research poll of American Christians revealed that only 21 percent view their knowledge of the Bible as mature, that more than double that number believe they are highly mature in maintaining healthy relationships.[1] For more and more American Christians of the mainline and Catholic churches, it seems, faith is about what you do, your therapeutic skills in relating to others, not about the content of the faith.

In fairness, it could be that the reasons why present American Christians are not as sanguine as their predecessors regarding Biblical knowledge is that in our fast-paced society with more options for entertainment, they just have not had the time the elders did for study. Everybody reads less today, no matter what the subject. But we cannot discount the likelihood that the critical approach to Scripture typical of mainline seminary education in the last half-century, coupled with the therapeutic vision of the faith that is largely espoused in those circles, has had an impact on American parishes.

Let's consider what happens when the therapeutic model dominates religious life. We are likely to gain from such an examination insights about what has happened to many segments of mainline American Christianity. This is politically significant for understanding what sorts of political overtures to Christians in the mainline Protestant and Catholic pews will be successful. And for those of us who want to free Jesus from the conservative stranglehold the Right has on Him, we need to understand these dynamics in order to appreciate why the laity in these churches are so susceptible to the Right's version of the Lord.

The insights of a celebrated Evangelical ecumenical consultant, Richard Quebedeaux, made almost twenty-five years ago remain most relevant today.[2] In his book *By What Authority*, he pointed out the shift of emphasis in much contemporary theological education from theological learning to a more practice-oriented approach to ministry. It is quite typical in almost every mainline Protestant seminary that the most popular courses are the ones devoted to the practice of ministry (preaching, counseling, or administration), without much attention to theology and

Biblical studies. The average parish pastor and priest have these predilections. And then, as a result of the dominance of the therapeutic, nonjudgmental ethos on many mainline seminary campuses, along with a general lowering of standards in most American educational institutions, it's not as hard to get through seminary as it was forty years ago. The assignments and tests aren't as rigorous (because "second-career students have so many demands on them," it is said) and even at Ivy League schools the grading system has given way to pass-fail grades (since evaluation is "threatening"). As a result, graduates don't learn as much.

Quebedeaux is on target in observing that the mainline churches do not have much depth, and that due to their emphasis on practice are more likely to be caught up in the spirit of capitalism. This is a fascinating insight that may help explain the co-option of much of American Christianity by the pro-business Right. And with this co-opting by those friendly with business, it is hardly surprising that business-management models dominate in much modern mainline church life, both at the congregational and especially at the national denominational level.

Without a preoccupation with the depth of knowledge, Quebedeaux contends that American religion is marked by a lack of depth, a superficiality that even permeates the kind of relationships it nurtures. This superficiality is present everywhere in most church circles—in the superficiality of professional relations among clergy (more in the mode of competition than friendship), in how they relate to parishioners, in the way in which those at the top of their denominations have cultivated relationships and networked to get there, and even in the superficiality of the marriage ideal today (evident in how readily divorce and shacking up are more and more acceptable in mainline church circles).

This stress on practice is evident, Quebedeaux notes, in an exhaustive study of ministry, which appeared in book form in 1980 titled *Ministry in America*. It illustrates that as early as the late 1970s, congregations were concerned primarily with personality/therapeutic gifts, not so much with spiritual gifts and theological skills. It is evident, other commentators have observed, that American religion has been personalized. But a personalized religion is not binding. It is about the self and his or her relationships.[3]

These priorities even reflect at the national denominational level. We previously noted how most of these denominations evaluate the personality of candidates for the ministry even more rigorously than they do the candidates' theological competence. And the average continuing education event for church leaders of these denominations is little occupied with theology, Biblical studies, or Church history. Nine out of ten such events will be about enhancement of skills pertaining to administration or counseling.

Quebedeaux also contends that the concern for relationships in mainline denominations is all a mask for the free-market individualism (we might call it narcissism) nurtured by mainline religion. For all the talk one hears about "community" in these churches, apart from a stress on content that binds people to a common heritage, what remains is myself and relationships that can benefit me. I need relationships *for myself*. But there is no communal history or long-term commitment to the community when the task of such community is so defined. Indeed, the Church community on these terms is more like the "team" concept of contemporary business management techniques: a flexible group of workers assembled for a specific task, but only on a temporary basis. A church like this nurtures self-centeredness. Rather than nurturing deep relationships, most of the time congregational life in many mainline Protestant and Catholic churches (except in "boondock" [true] communities where the members have grown up together and also play and work together) is relationally superficial.[4] We work together on committees and superficially socialize, but we do not share much except for therapeutic purposes. We are not really brothers and sisters or friends in Christ.

Even God takes a backseat in this therapeutic, team-management culture. We are only interested in God when belief in Him is meaningful or meets our needs. This leads to a casual approach to God, manifest in the marked decline in the dress codes for worship in mainline churches since the 1970s—even though we're not so casual in our attire for the job interview, first date, or Senior Prom.

Quebedeaux contends that mainline American religion's therapeutic ethos essentially buys the therapeutic, free-market hypothesis that people can and must do for themselves. The therapeutic ideal of acceptance and no guilt, even as it has been translated into the Church, has not become a word of grace (of justification by grace alone). A 2005 poll conducted by the Barna Research Group bears out this point, as it seems that more than half of all American adults (54 percent) believe that people who are good earn salvation. In 2000, 74 percent of Americans believed that the Bible teaches God helps those who help themselves. Although many mainline Protestant church members voted for Democratic candidates in 2006 (47 percent compared to 44 percent in 2004), this sort of optimistic piety focused on meeting individual needs lends itself to an openness to the pro-business interests of Republican politics.[5] The practical impact of the dominant theological paradigm of the mainline churches is to nurture more Republican voters, and those members rejecting the dominant theology may find no other alternatives than that of the Evangelical Movement and its endorsement of the political Right.

THE CURSE OF RELATIVISM

Just prior to his election to the papacy in 2005, Pope Benedict XIV identified relativism as *the* central problem of our time.[6] He is right. The relativism of the prevailing models of mainline theology, coupled with the relativism of the outlook on life propagated in the universities since World War II and by the media elite, as well as the therapeutic model for doing ministry (which reduces everything to my psychic well-being), have had their impact on American society and also on Christians in the American pews. A 2002 poll by the Barna Research Group revealed that by a three-to-one margin the American public regards moral truth as relative. Among teenagers and mainline Christians the margin is four out of five. (Even among Evangelicals there is still a bare majority of those denying absolute moral truth in favor of situational ethics.) These numbers are somewhat in line with an earlier 1991 survey of the Barna Group when the question pertained to absolute truth, and only one in three of the American public and one out of five among mainline Christians affirmed the possibility.[7]

This relativism in the pews explains a number of contemporary social and ecclesiastical dynamics. On one hand it helps explain the leadership crisis in mainline Protestant and Catholic congregations, where clergy are regularly in conflict with laity, often losing their appointments due to the conflicts.[8] Although for historic reasons it is not so much a problem in American Judaism, Christian pastors and priests do not have as much authority as they had in the past. What they say is now seen as just their opinion.

Another problem with the relativism relates to the new openness in mainline Protestant and Catholic churches, at least in these denominations' pews, to the ways of the world—a forfeiture of distinct Christian ethical commitments, like strictures against divorce, extramarital sex, and homosexuality.[9] This not only explains the Evangelical backlash to mainline ethics. It also helps account for why the mainline churches are not attending so much to economic injustices or the present war in Iraq, why—although members of these churches were a little more friendly to Democrats in 2006—they are still not advocating for the poor. It is more difficult to be prophetic against society's injustices when everything is relative, when everyone's opinion is equally valid. Only the Right's vision of Jesus and His Gospel seems to offer an alternative to what society is doing. But that vision offers little in the way of critiquing present economic or international affairs policies. Mainline Protestantism and Catholicism need to break with relativism if these American Christians want to find a way to offer a new alternative to the Right, one committed to justice and peace.

Speaking of ethics, the therapeutic mind-set aims to make us feel more confident in ourselves, with its role in abolishing shame and guilt. A good indication of the impact of this mind-set on contemporary American mainline church life is evident in the negative reactions mainline church pastors and priests are apt to hear when they preach on Sin. We have already noted poll results verifying this reality. Contrary to the doctrine of Original Sin, Americans seem to think they are good and can save themselves by their works. As we will see, this is another way in which American religion is going against the grain of core American (Constitutional) suppositions. It makes the religious convictions of mainline Christianity politically irrelevant in several ways. Our Constitutional system itself is not as optimistic about human nature, even if the Right's version of that heritage is not so clear about that matter. More of that in the concluding section of the book.

WHATEVER HAPPENED TO CHRISTIAN ADVOCACY OF SOCIAL JUSTICE AND ANTIPOVERTY CAMPAIGNS?

Also noteworthy in connection with the way in which American mainline Protestant and Catholic churches have been caught up in social trends of the media and cultural elite is the way in which these Protestant bodies have preoccupied themselves since the 1970s and 1980s with advocacy of women's rights and gay rights, while largely remaining silent about the growing imbalance of wages and the Right's ongoing crusade against Affirmative Action for racial minorities. In some respects, the neglect of these broader social justice issues seems to be at odds with the ethos of American academia. But not if we keep in mind the degree to which the academy has become infused with the therapeutic mind-set that focuses more on individual self-fulfillment and individual rights than justice for society as a whole.

There is another way in which these trends seem at odds with one of the basic suppositions of the academy since World War II—especially of the theology of the academy. The common sense of this culture has been if you want to be liberal on social and political issues, you need to have a Liberal Theology that is in dialogue with all these trends by means of a Method of Correlation in some sense. Obviously this is not the case with regard to the Liberal Theology of these mainline Protestant denominations, nor are theologically liberal Catholic theologians taking notably socially progressive positions, save perhaps those influenced by Liberation Theology. In fact, the major outcome of liberal theology seems to have been these churches' preoccupation with issues of personal well-being and individual rights, the sort of individualistic preoccupation that certainly does not challenge the preoccupation with individual behavior or the "family values" of the Religious Right.

Poll results suggest that this prioritizing of such issues at the national office level of the mainline churches has not been accepted by the members of these denominations. Exit polls by the Fourth National Survey of Religion and Politics for the 2004 election reveal that those mainline Protestants concerned with social issues strongly preferred Bush (58 percent to 42 percent). This indicates that much of these denominations' membership prefers the Republican platform on gays and abortion to their denominations' support of these matters. On the other hand, those members of mainline Protestant and Catholic churches who considered themselves socially liberal on moral issues, were concerned about the economy, and celebrated religious pluralism (i.e., relativism), while not too regularly attending worship, did support the Democrats (by 75 percent to 25 percent)—even a bit more of a majority for Kerry than their atheist and agnostic counterparts supported

Democratic candidates.[10] This was the group of mainline Protestants that accounts for why Bush's support from mainline Protestants fell slightly in 2004 compared to the percentage of such Christians supporting him in 2000. This group probably also accounts for the near standoff Democrats gained among white mainstream Protestant voters in 2006.[11]

The polls coupled with the 2004 election outcome data indicate that this liberal segment comprises only about one-third of the voting membership of these mainline churches. The majority of Catholics and a large portion of Protestant mainline denomination members attend church regularly and have a conservative theology, even to the point of being Biblical literalists (though there is a mixture of relativism in expressing an openness to the truth of other religions).[12] Democrats will not get elected by just appealing to the Religious Left.

WHAT IT MIGHT TAKE TO WIN BACK
THE PEWS FROM THE RIGHT

The implications of this data are clear. In order to recapture the mainline Protestant and Catholic vote, and to halt the further erosion of the black and Hispanic vote, the Democrats and the mainline denominations need a version of Jesus and His Gospel that can better communicate with the churchgoing, theologically conservative faithful. (This strategy could also be helpful in building bridges to Evangelicals.) But the present situation as we have been describing it finds mainline Protestant and Catholic churches engaged in just the opposite strategy. Rather than having an impact on the popular American psyche because of the social positions and theology that these churches embrace under the guise of being in step with the times, these churches are effectively further alienating American believers. Not only are the social positions advocated suspect to the Puritan piety of most American churchgoers. The critical approach to Scripture and relativist view of truth that undergird the prevailing streams of academic theology now propounded in the congregations also conflict with the literalistic piety of most American Christians (as nearly one in two Americans believe that the Bible is totally accurate in all its teachings).[13] It is evident that a new model for "doing Church" is required by the mainline and Catholic fellowships, new models, and methods for ministry.

The problems and directions have been sketched. Everything points to a more theologically conservative, socially liberal approach to theology and ministry, one that breaks with the unbridled free-market, individualistic orientation of the Revivalist-amended Puritan Paradigm, but still in touch with some of its core suppositions. Before we get to that in the final chapters, there are still some other things to be learned from why the mainline and Catholic churches have become so Republican, and why certain minority churches have not gotten into that pattern, but remained solidly Democrat. It is to that task we next turn.

A warning also needs to be appended at this point. The next chapters further highlight the complexity of the dynamics that have led to the Republican co-option of the faith. Just as this chapter highlights, what follows will point out why the process of reversing these trends will not be easy. It will take a whole new ethos of church life in the mainline Protestant denominations and the Catholic Church to turn things around, to get the laity to believe in Jesus' as well as the Father's (the created order's) disposition toward the poor and suspicion of unbridled power, and that won't come easy. But at least the data in this chapter and the next ones point us in a way to go.

7

The Impact of Americanization

Another reason for the influence of the Religious Right's individualized Puritan version of Christianity on all segments of American society has been the impact of the process of Americanization on certain denominations with a strong ethnic flavor in their origins.

As distinctly ethnic, these religious bodies (not just the Jewish community, but also Roman Catholic, Eastern Orthodox, and even many Lutheran denominations) had little incentive to side with the American establishment and its business interests, to become increasingly conservative and Republican. These dynamics especially became relevant during the Depression and the Roosevelt recovery, as immigrants were more likely to be hurt in this era and so became inclined to side with organized labor and the big-government public-works projects of the New Deal.

It was also in the Roosevelt era that the previously solid Republican loyalty of the African-American community (loyalty to the Party of Lincoln) began to erode in favor of support for New Deal programs, which were in the interest of many black Americans. Although a significant number of African-Americans especially in the South remained Republican into the 1940s, 1950s, and even early 1960s, during the Civil Rights Movement the vast majority came to align with the Democratic Party as a result of the perceived support of the Kennedy and Johnson administrations for their agendas, and the lack of support for civil rights by many Republican leaders. Many Asian-Americans, for analogous, but different reasons, made a similar shift from Republican to Democrat loyalties.[1] Inasmuch as these last two ethnic groups remain loyal to the Democrats, and so are stubborn exceptions to the trends noted in the previous chapters, we will examine them more fully in the next chapter.

Of course, as we noted, the biggest vote switch numerically seems to have come in Evangelical circles, in theologically conservative denominations like the Southern Baptist Convention in particular. (Its conversion to the Right was all part of the "Southern Strategy" of Republicans in the Nixon years, an attempt to build a coalition between the pro-business base of the Party, religiously inclined Americans, and voters in the South.) But this conversion was not about an ethnic body changing its stripes. This switch in voter loyalties was about a group of Christians who were born to American families of many generations (perhaps with ancestors who fought in the "War Between the States" [that's Southern talk], if not before). Their loyalty to the Democratic Party was not primarily about economics and the Party's stand on openness to immigrants. It was rather occasioned (especially in the South) by family traditions and the Party's identification with populism (not to mention, in the South, its support of segregation). These voters were conservative Democrats. This made them the perfect targets for the successful Southern Strategy, as the Republican Party successfully lured them away from the Democrats by appealing to their socially conservative values and distaste for big government, along with some racial overtones thrown in. But in this process, though there are important differences, there are analogies to the Americanization process in the case of Southern Baptists and related denominations.

Let's return to the story of the distinctively ethnic denominations we have noted, which moved into the Republican column in 2004, and even earlier than that in some cases. Exit polls reveal that Bush won the once strongly Democratic Catholic vote by a margin of 52 percent to 47 percent. White Catholics voted in an even higher proportion for Bush (by 56 percent to 43 percent). True enough, the 2006 Congressional election exit polls reveal a slight (1 percent) white Catholic majority for Democrats, but that seems more a function of antiwar, anticorruption, anti-Bush attitudes than anything else, just a reflection of national trends. Despite a Democratic—even Socialist—heritage from their native regions, exit polls for 2004 indicate that members of Orthodox churches voted Republican (almost by an eight out of ten margin).[2]

Although most German Lutherans were not originally friendly to labor unions, that began to change in the early twentieth century among

Americanized German Lutherans. (Many German Lutherans in Wisconsin who affiliated with the Wisconsin Evangelical Synod came to America as Socialists and so did affiliate with the Democratic Party.) Finnish Lutherans and Scandinavian (especially Norwegian) Lutherans became increasingly union friendly. But American Lutherans on the whole (again with Germans taking the lead) voted Republican in 2004. In fact, two of the three largest American Lutheran denominations, The Lutheran Church–Missouri Synod and the Wisconsin Evangelical Synod (abandoning their original immigrant heritage), both founded and fundamentally comprised of German Americans, have been voting Republican at least since 1972, even before the *Roe v. Wade* Supreme Court Ruling that legalized abortion.[3]

How are we to account for all these voter shifts of ethnically based denominations? Why have they shifted, and not African-American churches, Hispanic Catholics, and Scandinavian (especially Norwegian-American) Lutherans? The answer is complex, yet simple. Complex in the sense that all these denominations have changed markedly since their founding in America, in terms of their styles of worship, ministry, parish life, theology, and even inclusivity, as well as in educational level or social standing of their membership. Yet the changed voting patterns can also to some extent be summarized in one word (the same word that helps us understand the preceding changes): Americanization.

All of these denominations started on the outside of American society. With the exception of German Lutherans, they were not established in any significant numbers in the Colonial era. (It is true that the first Speaker of the House of Representatives, Frederick Muhlenberg [1750–1801], was the son of a prominent leader of this community, and there was at least one Lutheran delegate to the Constitutional Convention, Jacob Broom [1752–1810], who seems to have been Anglicized, if not of Scottish ethnicity.) Even these Germans were hardly mainstreamed in significant numbers. Most spoke a foreign language. And we must always remember that for over a century and one-half before the founding of our nation, English was the language of those in charge.

These Lutherans also did not blend into the dominant religious ethos of the Colonies—the Puritan Paradigm. They did not (do not) worship like Puritans. Their use of a fixed (Roman Catholic) liturgy, stress on Sacramental life, clerics who dressed like Catholics, and a theology that did not stress discipline set them apart from Puritans. (Similarities to Anglican ways of worship somehow went unnoticed by outside observers, and were not noticed by Lutheran immigrants themselves, although some later Americanized generations did, even to the point of joining The Episcopal Church.) The use of a foreign language in the worship made it clear to the average British colonist that they were a "foreign church." Although some Americanization did begin even in the Colonial era, as German gave way to English in worship in the older German settlements, new waves of immigrants, beginning in the nineteenth century (especially from Finland, Sweden, Denmark, and Norway) kept the Lutheran church a "foreign" institution until well into the twentieth century.

For reasons that will become subsequently clearer, the fact that Germans got a head start in Americanization before these other segments of American Lutheranism provides some hints regarding why they are more likely to vote Republican than Scandinavian-American segments of the Lutheran community. Another factor has been that a large segment of German Lutherans belong to The Lutheran Church–Missouri Synod and the Wisconsin Evangelical Lutheran Synod, denominations with a view of Scripture much like that of the Religious Right, which predisposes these Lutherans to embrace the Right's political agenda.

Much like Scandinavian Lutherans, the sense of being part of a foreign institution was even more pronounced with regard to the experience of Eastern Orthodox Christians, Catholics, and Jews in America. All of these populations did not arrive in any numerical bulk until the nineteenth century (especially after the Civil War), spoke a foreign tongue, and hailed from parts of Europe or Asia that were even more culturally distinct from the dominant English-speaking Protestants of the early Republic. In short, they were "those people." Unlike the Lutheran immigrant population, they could never blend in with the Anglos (unless they married into such families and their kids could "pass"). And when it comes to their church style, they were even more at odds with the Puritan Paradigm, even with regard to authority in the Church (as these churches opted for bishops with much authority). As for Jews, they bore all the ethnic "challenges" we have observed in the other groups noted, and on top of that they were practicing another religion.

All these groups have remained out of the mainstream through most of their history, even after the sons and daughters of the immigrants learned American English. In several cases, at least the Lutherans, the Orthodox Christians, and certain Catholics (the Irish and Germans, and maybe even some Italians) could blend in, as they looked like the American majority. But some of them for a long time preferred to live among "their own kind," which further kept them out of the mainstream.

They also were alienated from the American mainstream in that they still did not have a religious approach like real (Puritan) America. We can observe this distancing from the American mainstream by reminding ourselves that none of these religious groups has ever elected a President, save Kennedy the Irish Catholic. (A Greek Orthodox member [Mike Dukakis] has headed a ticket, at least one Jew was a running mate [Joe Lieberman], and another Catholic [John Kerry] almost won.) But that's it. These groups have been removed from the center of power. Even today, while the 110th Congress has only seventeen Lutheran Congressmen in office and there are five Eastern Orthodox members in Congress, churches associated with the Puritan Paradigm hold 222 Congressional seats (only three of them Southern Baptists). That is still far more than the forty-three Jewish Congressmen. Even the largest American denomination, the Roman Catholic Church, totals nearly seventy Congressional seats less than the smaller denominations affiliated with the Puritan Paradigm. (These are all-time high numbers of Representatives and Senators for these religious bodies.)

Enough said: If you want to be President, and even if you want to go to Congress, don't join (and be sure you don't get born into) a Jewish synagogue or a Catholic, Lutheran, Mormon, or Eastern Orthodox church. You are off to a bad start belonging to those religious bodies and their associated ethnicities. With some exceptions (we think of the Jewish business establishment and Mormons, at least in Utah), for national purposes the real political and even business contacts are likely to come in Episcopalian, Presbyterian, U.C.C. [Congregationalist], Methodist, and Baptist churches. The history of the other religious bodies to which you might belong won't have as many educated members, at least until recently, and not as much "old money." On top of that, if you ever run for political office, you will have to spend a lot of time explaining your "unusual" religious convictions to the public. Not so many questions will be raised if you're Episcopalian, Methodist, Baptist, or Congregationalist.

There is a lesson to be learned here for the Democrats regarding the traditional religious affiliation of these ethnic groups and religious bodies.

(It is a lesson that these religious bodies also need to learn about their heritage in America in order to guide preaching and teaching today.) All of them until recently (save the bulk of German Lutherans) were solid Democratic constituencies since the rise of organized labor movements and Roosevelt's New Deal era. The reason: Except for its support of states' rights (in order to protect small farmers from the federal government and its business interests from imposing high tariffs on their agricultural produce, which regrettably opened the door for retaining slavery and later segregation), Democrats have been on the side of the little guy over and against the interests of big business. This is why, with just a few exceptions, until the rise of Religious Right and the Clinton New Democrat strategy, immigrants, the labor force, and others marginalized in some way from the American establishment (including those who were members of religious bodies not belonging to the Puritan Paradigm) voted Democrat. But now, at least in the case of churchgoing Catholics, Eastern Orthodox Christians, and German Lutherans, most of them vote Republican. They have all gotten Americanized, as the Puritan Paradigm has had some significant impact on their religious communities.

HOW AMERICANIZATION HELPS
MAKE GOOD REPUBLICANS

All of these communities have gotten Americanized as the last wave of European immigrants who spoke the mother language died out. (The exception here is in the Catholic Church, which has grown by leaps and bounds of late with the large wave of Hispanic immigration.) Even in their own religious communities, these ethnic religious groups have increasingly converted to English worship, even the Catholics since the Second Vatican Council (just like the Puritans and the Revivalists).

These language developments opened the door to more opportunities for younger generations. And a key for opportunity is education. Yes, education may expose the young to some Left-Wing ideology, at least on college campuses. But for various reasons I've outlined in more detail in another book, the German Enlightenment relativistic ethos they learn there doesn't take. The students mouth the words to get through the system, but their real interests are in careers they can have when they graduate.[4] And once they graduate, these young adults get better jobs than their less educated parents; they are more likely to become part the American establishment.

One of the untold stories of American religion's turn to the Right has been the rising level of American Christianity (particularly these denominations outside the Puritan Paradigm's mainline denominations) with regard to education and socioeconomic class. Sociologist Robert Wuthnow pointed out that between 1960 and 1976, Catholics moved from only being 80 percent as likely as the general population to hold a professional or managerial position, to being just as likely as any American male to hold such a job. Likewise, in this period they moved from being 0.7 as likely as any American to have gone to college, to being above the national average of college graduates.

Lutherans were almost as successful in social class ascent. In the same period they moved from only being 60 percent as likely as the population as a whole to hold professional or managerial jobs to a 90 percent likelihood. Correspondingly, they increased from 0.7 to 0.9 as likely as any American to be a college graduate.[5]

Some other dynamics transpired in these religious communities, which further Americanized them. Even before some of these socioeconomic and educational gains went into effect (in the case of Lutherans dating back to the nineteenth century), these bodies took on characteristics of the American Revivalist version of the Puritan Paradigm—in a more pronounced way of course among Lutherans, who are in some sense Protestant—than Catholics and Orthodox. There are some Eastern Orthodox families that celebrate Christmas (culturally) on December 25 with the rest of America, even though the Eastern date is January 6. And so you are likely to be told in the company of some members of this community that, "We celebrate Christmas twice."

Catholic life is a lot different since the 1960s. We have already referred to the move away from Latin. But although the liturgical and Sacramental life remains in place in most parishes, some accommodations to the American version of the Puritan Paradigm are in evidence. Weekly confession of sins and a no-meat diet on Fridays is out. You don't even have to give up anything for Lent. (It's like the Puritans, who don't really observe the season.) And as for worship, Catholics now sing Revivalist hymns (in some parishes). Even speaking in tongues, as happens sometimes among Religious Right leaders like Pat Robertson, can transpire in Catholic circles since Vatican II. Doctrinally, leading

Catholic theologians in America (like in the rest of world) now say that they teach about salvation very much the way Protestants do—by grace.[6]

The Americanizing of Lutheranism by adopting aspects of the Puritan Paradigm began in America even in Colonial times. We have already noted that, partly due to a lack of enough clergy to be present for worship in each parish each week and due to the influence of Pietism on several Lutheran churches in Europe, but also because of the pressures of the Puritan Paradigm, the Sacramental character of historic Lutheranism was severely compromised. Along with it, liturgical worship was virtually lost at several times during American Lutheran history. Even the distinct Lutheran emphasis on justification by grace and freedom from the Law (see the Lutheran Smalcald Articles, II.I) has sometimes been compromised by American Lutherans embracing in a very Puritan way the importance of discipline and the continuing obligation Christians have to obey God's Law.[7]

These aspects of the Lutheran heritage might have been lost had it not been for various waves of European immigrants who did not Americanize as quickly, did not succumb to the Puritan Paradigm, and as a result moved the more Americanized part of the Lutheran constituency back to its roots. (It is interesting to speculate if new waves of immigration might begin to do that to the American branches of the Catholic and Orthodox churches.) And although this nineteenth–early-twentieth-century immigration wave has kept many historic Lutheran affirmations "on the books," in recent decades their vibrancy has become increasingly fragile. Visit some Lutheran congregation sometime, and you may observe a very American-like, Puritan style of worship (done in the twenty-first-century mode of informality). Recent 2001 poll results by the Barna Research Group indicate that despite the historic stress on salvation by grace alone, Lutherans are less likely to affirm that works play no role in earning heaven than Presbyterians or the national average (a paltry 27 percent for Lutherans as compared to a no less pathetic 31 percent and 30 percent for Presbyterians and the American public, respectively).[8]

Isn't it interesting? As the membership of these bodies gets more Americanized, church life takes on more characteristics of the Puritan Paradigm (an amended Puritanism with little use for grace and the sovereignty of God). And as that has transpired in varying degrees at least just a bit in the case of the Lutheran, Catholic, and Eastern Orthodox traditions, the members of these denominations have voted Republican, and so become more friendly to business interests. This seems to be a chicken-and-egg matter regarding which comes first—whether Americanization precedes the endorsing of the ways of the Puritan Paradigm in your religious community or whether changing your religious mores aids Americanization. It does not matter.

There is a lesson in this for the church leader concerned to avoid nurturing a conservative Jesus. At least in the case of these traditions, and others not comfortably situated in the Puritan Paradigm, one way to avoid proclaiming this Jesus and the gospel of Bush is to be sure not to compromise the distinctive traits of your heritage. We will elaborate on that point further in the next chapter as we examine further relevant exit poll and sociological data.

These trends were nicely illustrated by the Catholic vote in 2004. Previously cited exit polls by the Fourth National Survey of Religion and Ethics indicated that the more Americanized its constituency has become the more it has voted Republican, despite its earlier union loyalties (by 52 to 47 percent). The numbers were even higher among white (presumably more Americanized) Catholics (56 to 43 percent). But the untold story relates to Hispanics and Hispanic Catholics. According to the same exit poll Hispanic Catholics supported Kerry by almost seven out of ten.[9]

Of course, some analysts would point out that the shift in the Catholic vote over the last decades is closely related to the evaluation of the Democratic Party as the Pro-Choice Party. But that thesis does not take into account 2005 Gallup poll results indicating that over one-third of American Catholics deem abortion morally acceptable. (As early as 1992, one-half the Catholic membership deemed homosexuality as morally acceptable.)[10] The claim that the shift in Catholic voting patterns is a function of Democratic policies related to sexuality also does not explain either why at least half of white Catholics voted Democratic in 2006, or the continued loyalty of Hispanic Catholics to Democrats. Americanization is the most plausible way of interpreting the new Republican voting patterns among Catholics.

Despite losing the Hispanic Catholic vote in 2004, Bush won by a slight margin the Hispanic Protestant vote (by just over six out of ten).

(No statistics are yet available on the 2006 Hispanic Protestant vote.) We may see here again the importance of the Puritan Paradigm, as these Hispanic Protestants largely belong to Puritan-like churches, while Hispanic Catholics remain affiliated with a very "un-American" religious tradition—a tradition of ritual and other doctrinal commitments—that does not fit readily with characteristic Puritan-Revivalist beliefs. The same dynamics may help explain the continuing Jewish preference for Democrats (by nearly three out of four in 2004, by nearly nine in ten in 2006). More about these statistics in the next chapter.

HOW THE SOUTH AND RURAL AMERICA GOT REPUBLICAN AND AMERICANIZED AT THE SAME TIME: IS IT JUST A COINCIDENCE?

Some of these dynamics help us sort out some of the dynamics (ones usually overlooked by analysts) involved in the success of the Republican strategies to win the support of certain Southern-based denominations associated with the Evangelical Movement (especially the Southern Baptist Convention). The regionalism of the South and rural areas elsewhere in the nation, which were the bastion of post-Scopes Trial Fundamentalism and the early Evangelical Movement, should not be forgotten. Prior to the end of segregation and the corresponding creation of the "exurbs" (the erection of upscale homes in formerly rural pockets beyond the existing suburbs), the South and rural America were regarded as the "boondocks." To come from these regions was, in a sense, to be perceived as out of the American mainstream (at least among the elite bastions of American culture, not to mention in the streets of Brooklyn). Southern kids and college students from the South always had to apologize for their origins and accents if they attended elite (and even not-so-elite) Northern schools or worked in Northern businesses.

It is not as much of a cross to bear to come from the South or rural America anymore—at least if it's Atlanta, Charlotte, the Poconos, or Iowa. There has also been enough immigration from the elite echelons to these regions to level off the regionalization of these areas. This Yankee immigrant has to wait for a while to hear a Southern accent in metropolitan Atlanta sometimes.

All of these dynamics contribute to an explanation of why residents of these regions, why members of the churches of the Evangelical Movement from these regions, are now voting Republican. No less that the ethnic-based churches we have examined, theologically conservative rural and Southern Christians, are now part of the American mainstream. And, as we have seen, when you become part of the mainstream you tend to get more saturated with the Puritan Paradigm than ever before. And that predisposes you to vote for free-market capitalism, along with the empathy your conservative moral views lead you to have with Republican candidates espousing such views.

Even if you are a Southerner who lives in regions that are still undesirable as the media and the cultural elite spin it, alignment with Republicanism still has its attractions, not just because it represents your conservative moral values. To be aligned with the elite, especially if the elites in question are "good people," is quite attractive to those on the "outside." (This dynamic explains why many poor whites sided with the rich Southern establishment's institution of segregation after the failure of Reconstruction. It also explains why some African-Americans embraced Puritan styles of worship.) I may be from the rural backwoods, but I get to be somebody by associating with a highbrow like you, especially if you are religious like me and seem to share a lot of my values. And when you tell me that a free market creates opportunities, even for someone like me, I'm more likely to sign on and vote for you. Americanization further encourages people from the outside to want to become Republican.

WHERE DO WE GO FROM HERE?

It will be a losing battle if Democrats just rely on those not caught up in the Puritan Paradigm, not thoroughly Americanized. There are certainly not enough votes to win if the constituency is the Secularists and those outside the mainstream. We may gain some insights about strategies from examining those segments of the American religious population outside the mainstream—somewhat ethnic, but still loyal to Democratic agendas. Let's take a look.

8

Stubborn Exceptions to the Trends and What They Might Teach Us

You have already had your attention called to the fact there have been some segments of American Christianity that have resisted the trends we have been noting. Especially Christians in the African-American community, Hispanics (especially Hispanic Catholics), Scandinavian (especially Norwegian) Lutherans, and some segments of the Asian-American community have continued to or begun to vote Democratic. If we widen the analysis to include groups with many adherents of other religions, we should include Jews and Arab-Americans. Only 44 percent of Hispanics supported Bush, 44 percent of Asian-Americans, 11 percent of African-Americans, 29 percent of Arab-Americans, and 25 percent of Jews supported Bush in 2004. In the 2006 elections, the numbers favoring Democrats were even higher: Hispanics 69 percent, African-Americans 91 percent, and Jews 87 percent.[1]

Common sense and insights gained in the previous chapter help us identify what all of these groups have in common. To some extent, they have not fully "Americanized," not adopted or been allowed to integrate fully into American ways of life, achieved at least a middle-class lifestyle, and/or do not practice a religion that fits with the Puritan Paradigm. An analysis of these dynamics can provide Democrats with some insights about what it will take to build a broad coalition that includes all of these minorities, without losing either their secular base or the broader Americanized voting public that belongs to the Puritan Paradigm.

Of course, the ethnic character of these segments of American religion, their failure to blend into the mainstream, clearly encourages political commitments that do not support the American business establishment.

But although this insight is a reminder to religious leaders of these traditions that failing to retain some appreciation of their ethnic roots as Americanization impacts the membership (as it inevitably will) is to invite the conservative Jesus and the Right's version of the Gospel to take root in that church, it is also not a good political strategy. For one item, there are simply not enough votes among those outside the establishment to win national elections. And even if there were, it is unlikely that this constituency alone could provide enough money to win the elections. Once the richer candidate won the image battle in the media, it is likely he or she could lure enough minorities and others estranged from the mainstream to get elected.

Be it by a priest, pastor, or rabbi, it is not good pastoral care to impede Americanization. That would be like condemning parishioners to lives of powerlessness, if not poverty. My point is simply to suggest that a choice does not need to be made, that one can Americanize an ethnic religious community and still retain pride in and love for one's roots. The African-American Church, at least those segments of it that have embraced Afro-Centric and black pride strategies, is a good example of this middle ground. While celebrating African roots and distinct (non-Puritan) African-American ways of worship, many of these congregations also stress education and mastering "the King's English" in order to succeed in the world. A nationwide survey of congregational life conducted in 2000 revealed that one in two African-American congregations were committed to preservation of their racial/ethnic heritage (the second highest percentage of congregations, bested only by Hispanic congregations, which score over three out of five ranking this a high priority). But it also seems that about one in three offer tutoring opportunities.[2] To keep alive your ethnic roots does not preclude efforts to Americanize your membership. Is it not interesting that the Black Church and Hispanic congregations that prioritize preserving ethnic heritage continue to vote Democrat? Keep in mind that Jews are doing that too, while Scandinavian (especially Norwegian) Lutherans (that segment of the Lutheran constituency that has maintained the strongest ethnic roots) also vote Democrat.

In this connection, it is worth noting that in the 2004 election cycle Republicans made inroads on the African-American and Jewish communities (a 3 percent rise in the black community and a 5 percent rise among Jews).[3] Insofar as the largest rise was among the most religiously orthodox segments of these communities, it is worth noting that the support for Bush was occasioned by convergence at the level of certain personal values with the Right without consideration of how those values relate to their own communities. When being religious in your politics is divorced from your ethnic communal roots, from how your religio-political beliefs cash out for the advancement of your own community, you are operating with a kind of individualistic faith like the Revivalist tradition. And when that happens, you are on the way to the small-government, laissez-faire-policies agenda of the Right. Lesson one for religious and political leaders from the stubborn exceptions to the recent election trends: Maintain your connections to your ethnic or native religious heritage, because then your religious convictions will be less likely to degenerate into what is just good for individuals or for yourself. Religious leaders, heads up: In a way, provincialism facilitates universalism. Former Democratic Speaker of the House Tip O'Neil had it right: All (good Democratic) politics must be local.

Don't get me wrong. Not all ethnic-based denominations maintained loyalty to organized labor and the Democrats. The Dutch-rooted Christian Reformed Church is a notable exception of an ethnic denomination that was pro-capitalist and antiunion early in its history.[4] I suggest that although historical accidents of where these immigrants settled (mostly in the Midwest) and their social position cannot be discounted, the similarities between their Reformed-Calvinist theology and the Puritan Paradigm of America rendered it more natural for them to endorse the ways of the American establishment than it was for the ethnic denominations we have been discussing whose heritage is in tension with the Puritan Paradigm and American Revivalism. Another lesson: The more your heritage is in line with the Revivalist-amended Puritan Paradigm, the more readily it and the Republican agenda can co-opt your politics.

The very fact that Judaism is a distinct religion, clearly distinct from the Puritan Paradigm when it is truly practiced, helps explain why the Jewish vote continues to be a stubborn exception to present voting trends. Religious convictions of the Jews and their culture insulate them. Public policy couched in Puritan-Revivalist justifications may even be greeted with greater skepticism in this distinct religious ethos.

But what are the factors that insulate African-American Christians and Asian-American Protestants from the Republican appeal in view of the fact that the prevailing religious commitments of these ethnic groups are largely Puritan? It has to do with the correlation of the history of these groups and the way in which the Democratic Party has appealed to them. Let's clarify these matters in order to learn more lessons from the stubborn exceptions to the latest Republican victories and the Right's packaging of religion.

LEARNING MORE SENSITIVITY TO MINORITY CONCERNS

This last observation makes it all the more interesting that the African-American Church and Asian-American Protestants have embraced or continue to embrace Democratic loyalties. We start with unique aspects of the black experience, with what Democrats can learn about continuing to woo this constituency. Such concerns need to be on the front-burner, in view of some erosion of black voter support in previous election cycles. We also may be able to universalize these insights, to learn from them, in reaching out to other potential constituencies.

Distinguished African-American commentators on the black community like Cornel West and Anthony Pinn have pointed out several characteristics of the experience of that community that simply have to be taken into account because (in West's phrase), "Race Matters."[5] Collectively they point out several characteristics of the black experience that have ensued as a result of the experiences of slavery and racism. It is not a pretty picture. But politicians and religious leaders need to hear this message, lest we go the way the Right has in contending that the struggle for civil rights has been won. That's why we don't need Affirmative Action and reparations. A lot of Democrats and church leaders think that way too—the ones co-opted by the conservative Jesus. The insights of West and Pinn sing a different tune, which can safeguard against these developments.

The two analysts agree that in addition to addressing the curse of black poverty, we need to be sensitive to the role of racism in defining African-American self-identity negatively. This dynamic has not just had the effect of keeping African-Americans out of the mainstream and undergirded impeding the Americanization process we have described. But because others in the media portray who African-Americans are, marketing negative images that imply that blacks are not like the majority, a kind of self-loathing in the black community has tragically resulted. Merely enhancing economic opportunities does not rectify this experience, and as long as this is not recognized in political and religious policies, both the political parties and the religious community in question can expect a less enthusiastic and welcoming response in the black community. Alas these issues have not been on the radar screen of Democrats or of most of the mainstream Protestant and Catholic churches.

As a result of the failure of the Civil Rights Movement and desegregation to address these matters or to eliminate black poverty, West points out that the African-American experience today is characterized today by paralyzing pessimism and stultifying cynicism. Yet he still insists on the importance of Affirmative Action, without which there would be less chance of black access to prosperity.

These dynamics help us further to understand why, despite many economic and social gains and their involvement in churches that are part of the Puritan Paradigm, even middle-class African-Americans still vote Democratic. There are also lessons here for what Democrats (and churches) must do to ensure continuing African-American support and to meet African-American needs. Any compromise of commitment to eliminating black poverty and lessening the commitment to Affirmative Action (as we have seen transpire in both the post-Clinton Democratic Party and in the mainline denominations' political agendas) will lessen black support or be perceived by the Brothers and Sisters as a decline of interest in the African-American community. But West and Pinn also teach us that a Democratic Party and a Church committed to the black cause will also find ways to address African-American despair, which is closely related to ensuring more opportunities for black leadership and black self-definition. Republican efforts in the Bush era to place some African-Americans in high-profile administrative positions and to talk the language of black self-help may be perceived by some in the black community as a sensitivity to these yearnings. But they will not ultimately address the yearnings of the sons and daughters of Africa. Respect for African-American cultural roots is the sine qua non today for those who would be friends of that community.

The new Asian-American gravitation toward voting Democrat is a different dynamic. This community's voting exceptionalism, as has been observed by commentators, is of a different species than the African-American failure to blend into the melting pot.[6] And yet there is enough of a similarity to suggest that what the Democrats do to attract the black vote can also attract Asian-Americans.

Commentators Tamar Jacoby and Steve Sailer observe first that many in the Asian community are foreign born. And of course the Democratic Party has always been the party of immigrants. This has not been universally the case, though, in the Asian community, Jacoby notes. Chinese and Vietnamese Americans are said to lean toward the Republican Party, partly because of the GOP's stronger anti-Communism during their years in the homeland. For these reasons, and because of their high levels of educational accomplishment and entrepreneurial successes, as well as the income levels of many professionals, they tended to settle in largely Republican areas until 2000, though by 1996 their support for Republican laissez-faire policies was starting to wane.

Japanese and Filipinos, it seems, were longtime Democrat loyalists (possibly because they were not put off by stronger federal government policies sponsored by the Party). What seems to have begun to swing the Asian-American community as a whole in the direction of Democrats was the Party's commitment to diversity (an unwillingness to support Republican efforts to limit immigration), opposition to welfare cuts that affected new immigrants, and as a result of the experience of some younger Asian immigrants with the glass ceiling in business, the Democratic advocacy of Affirmative Action. To a great extent, this is the same winning formula for attracting African-American loyalties. When we add that Jewish reasons for Democratic loyalty are quite similar, it is clear that any diminution of these convictions in order to attract white-collar professionals who are socially liberal will not broaden the coalition it will take to stop the Right. Democrats and mainline church leaders objecting to the Republican version of faith have a lot to learn from the stubborn exceptions to present trends.

It is also significant that at least in the case of Jewish Americans, but also for Arab-Americans and Asian-Americans who are not Christian, and Hispanic Americans who are Catholic, the Republican marriage of its policies and the teachings of Christianity is also not likely to attract these constituencies. Indeed, no less than how it might be heard by the

Jewish community, a public policy proposal invoking Protestant (Puritan) beliefs for justification is likely to be viewed with some suspicion from a Muslim, Hindu, or even a Roman Catholic perspective. However, as the 2004 election taught us, it is incorrect with respect to African-Americans, as well as for the electorate as a whole, to conclude that the best strategy for Democrats is to keep religion out of their politics. On this matter as well, the African-American experience has relevance for teaching us further lessons.

THE ROLE OF RELIGION IN STAYING CLEAR OF THE RIGHT'S VISION FOR AMERICA

Another factor in the resistance to trends associated with the Right's views of Jesus is evident in the African-American community's religiosity and its characteristic theology. More African-Americans regularly attend church than any other ethnic group.[7] Though some proponents of Black Theology might differ, the view of Biblical authority that black Christians characteristically hold is more akin to the Right's literalism, than the mainline reliance on the relativistic assumptions of the Method of Correlation.[8]

However, the Biblical literalism of the Black Church is not the literalism of the Right and the Puritan Paradigm. Although exit polls indicate that Biblical literalism and frequent church attendance make you more likely to vote Republican,[9] the Evangelical Movement's construal of Scripture is tied to an affirmation (a theory) of Biblical infallibility. The problem with sublimating Scripture to a theory about the Bible, as Fundamentalism and the rest of Right has, is that the theory can readily transplant what the Biblical text actually says.

Good examples of this are evident in the Right's preoccupation with a handful of Biblical passages that seem to condemn abortion (Exodus 21:22–25; Psalm 139:13–16) and homosexuality (Leviticus 18:22; Romans 1:23–27; 1 Corinthians 6:9–10). Determined to protect the (infallible) authority of the Bible at all costs, the Family Values Coalition rarely attends to the fact that Jesus never condemned these activities against which its proponents so fervently contend. Nor with their preoccupation with theories of Biblical authority do they bother with the historical-critical and literary analysis of the text that suggest that neither premeditated medical abortion procedures nor committed gay and lesbian relations are condemned in these texts. Rather, the references to life in the womb seem poetic, the penalties imposed on causing a miscarriage pertain to the outcome of a fight, and the references to homosexuality seem to relate to strictures against one-night stands or prostitution. Look up the texts yourself. I have no agenda here. In the last chapters, you'll see that I want to have us solve these disputes by appeal to reason, not to invoke faith and the Bible.

No, we need a literalistic approach that actually takes the Biblical text as a whole into account, like the Black Church has. It will take such a literalism to prod the faithful to consider Bible verses that call Christians, Jews, and Muslims to concern for the poor with a conservative personal ethic. Get a Bible concordance, and look up the word "poor." Jim Wallis, in his book *God's Politics*, as well as the Black Church are right. Jesus and the Prophets have a real hang-up about serving the poor and overcoming poverty (Psalm 74:19; Proverbs 14:21; Isaiah 41:17; Zecharaiah 7:9–10; Matthew 19:21; Galatians 2:10).

The stubborn exceptions to the Right's capturing of American religious life teach that it will take a conservative, literalistic theology to recover a politically liberal Jesus. But how does that help us build a new liberal coalition (rebuild the old one)? Pastors and political consultants need to get clear on what this vision of Christian faith would look like. But before we get to that task, let's learn more from the Black Church's heritage.

In fact, the Biblical literalism in large segments of the Black Church and of other traditions not so ensconced in Enlightenment Relativistic thinking (especially Finnish and Norwegian Lutheranism in the Midwest and traditional Catholics who supported Kerry by a margin of nearly two out of three) is also a factor in keeping these religious adherents free from the Right's version of religiosity. Such a viewpoint puts the faithful in touch with a version of faith that is not affected by modern American preoccupations with individual well-being, self-fulfillment, and confidence in human goodness. These characteristics offer significant insights into what it might take for American Christianity as a whole (and other religious people) to recover a politically liberal version of the Gospel.

To repeat: A literalist approach to Scripture is not necessarily identical with the Fundamentalist, Puritan vision of the infallible Bible. But there are enough similarities to the Puritan model that this alternative literalism is more friendly to the politics of the Left and does allow its proponents to speak the (theological) language of conservativism embedded in and defined by the Puritan Paradigm. Such a Biblical literalism that we'll begin to flesh out has the makings of the foundation for a broader coalition.

Of course, a reminder of the realities of implementing all this needs to be made. Given the realities of present-day mainline Protestant and Catholic theological education, of church life in these denominations, and of the present attitudes of Democratic political consultants, it won't come easily or happen overnight. But turnarounds can begin with significant minorities, and that base already exists at the ballot box, in the American pews, and even in the theological academy. Let's flesh out what the vision and policies of that coalition might look like.

III

IT WILL TAKE A CONSERVATIVE THEOLOGY AND A NEW LIBERAL COALITION TO RECOVER A POLITICALLY LIBERAL JESUS

Resources in Classical Christianity

What are the classical themes that Christians need to stress in order to get Jesus and His Gospel back from the Republicans, in order to forge coalitions that can win elections? As we have been observing in the book, with some exceptions the Puritan impact on the Right has led it to emphasize WWJD ("What Would Jesus Do?") and other distinct Christian teachings. In an effort to take Jesus and His Gospel away from the Right, it will not be necessary—nor would it be wise—to challenge classical Christian formulations, as Liberal Theology, Feminist Theology, and Liberation Theology have done. To do so would be to create doubts among Christian voters. In fact, it is no accident that the two Christian thinkers with a Left-Wing agenda with perhaps the most impact on American politics in the twentieth century, Martin Luther King Jr. (1929–1968) and Reinhold Niebuhr (1892–1971), operated with fairly conservative theological assumptions.[1]

In this chapter I will demonstrate that the classical Christian tradition, along with the U.S. Constitution, provide plenty of fodder for progressive politics. Where do we start? For the sake of respecting the First Amendment, finding a way to build a broader coalition beyond just the faithful, and because I think there are richer, more appropriate political resources in the doctrines I will emphasize, I shall not take a Puritan approach to justifying a liberal politics by appealing to Jesus' teachings. On this one I am taking issue with Jim Wallis, who in his best seller, *God's Politics*, has called for incorporating "spiritual values" in our politics, with Randall Balmer and Bob Edgar, who in different ways take their bearings for a liberal politics from Jesus' distinct teachings in his Sermon on the Mount (Matthew 5–7), and also with Michael Lerner, who in his *The Left Hand of God* has called for a "spiritual politics" and a "spiritual covenant" with America, wanting love to be reflected in our social structures.[2] Instead, I am directing us to the doctrines of Creation (the natural law) and Sin as starting points for a politics of the Left. In that sense I am joining Bill Press (*How the Republicans Stole Christmas*), Jimmy Carter (*Our Endangered Values*), and Barack Obama (*The Audacity of Hope*). But none of them quite has it right, as Press fails to appreciate the impact of the natural law on U.S. law, and Carter and Obama do not expressly refer to the natural law, and neither say anything about Sin and its reflection in the Constitution.[3]

Although a stress on these themes is a break with the Puritan Paradigm, these are all themes affirmed by Puritanism, and sometimes even appeal to the natural law can be identified in that tradition. Let's clarify these themes, starting with the natural law. More self-conscious appropriation of the natural law tradition is a nice middle-ground way for the Democratic Party to "get religion" without risk of offending its Secular and Jewish constituency, a way to reject Puritan theocratic tendencies while still remaining squarely traditional in general.

THE NATURAL LAW

First, let's clarify what the natural law is. It is an ancient concept. In the minds of some legal scholars it is the heart of American—if not Western—jurisprudence. At the very least, Jefferson even conceded the compatibility between the Decalogue as the law of reason (the natural law) and the common law on which the American system was based.[4]

As previously suggested, the essence of the concept of the natural law is the claim that all people know the difference between right and wrong, that the core content of this moral sense is identical with many of the Ten Commandments. But for Christians, Jews, and Muslims, this common moral sense is a Work of God, the result of God structuring the created order in accord with His moral Commandments. In principle, then, this is a religious concept, one that the Democrats could endorse and expressly appeal to as a norm for their policies in order to "get religion." In this day of niche marketing, when it is deemed by marketers not to be productive to mass-market political and business products, targeting the concept of the natural law shared by all these traditions would allow Democrats to "spin" their proposals and values to this broad constituency while still seeking to target the particular interests and concerns of each of these religious constituencies.[5]

Of course, on grounds of the natural law, even nonreligious people have the capacity of doing God's Will. Consequently, an appeal to the natural law as the root and norm for political judgments does not preclude all Americans from political discourse. Unlike the drift of the Republicans' established Puritanism, which tends to privilege uniquely Christian values, appeals to the natural law do not entail that religious people have special insights about affairs of state. It is obvious, then, that doing politics from a natural law perspective is more in accord with the First Amendment. Indeed, as we shall see, it was from this perspective that the First Amendment was articulated. However, the perspective I am advocating does not relegate religion to a "hobby," as the brilliant Yale law professor Stephen Carter has lamented.[6]

Of course, it is true that the phrase "natural law" does not have a religious connotation in jurisprudence. There is no necessary reference to a God Who created our shared sense of right and wrong. As a result, some pundits like Bill Press and Ray Suarez have concluded that the Ten Commandments have little to do with the version of the natural law that underlies American jurisprudence.[7] This assumption is understandable insofar as the concept of natural law has had both sacred and secular origins. But, as we shall, see, Press's and Suarez's conclusions cannot be substantiated.

Historical Origins of the Concept

Something like the concept of the natural law can be identified in ancient Greek and Roman philosophy. Plato claimed that justice is in place both in individuals and in society where reason rules. He also contended that this higher order should be a framework for evaluating and making decisions about whether to accept the ethos of the republic. Aristotle made an even stronger case for the role of the natural law in critiquing laws of community.[8] Cicero, the great Roman orator and politician of the first century BC, actually appealed to an eternal law to critique certain hypothetical legislation of the Caesars of Rome. Marcus Aurelius, the Stoic philosopher who also became Emperor, appealed to a world-law known by reason, from which laws derive.[9]

The early Christian Church, no doubt indebted to these insights, more formally developed the concept, providing it with express religious connotation. One of the problems faced by these early Christians was what to make of the Mosaic law—whether it was still valid. Among the most impressive theologians of the first centuries of the Christian era was a martyr named Justin. He argued that Christians retained in the Mosaic law whatever was "*naturally* good, pious, and righteous." Other Church Fathers of the same era also referred expressly to the natural law.[10]

Later in this era, one of the most renowned theologians of the early Church, Origen (ca. 185–ca. 254), drew on a distinction made by adherents of Stoicism between "the ultimate law of nature" and "the written code of cities" to justify Christian refusal to obey idolatrous laws of the nations. The greatest theologian of the Western church, St. Augustine (354–430), whose theology we shall see deeply influenced America's Founders without many of them recognizing it, also spoke of the law written on our heart. All temporal laws, he claimed, must be derived from the eternal law based on reason.[11]

In the Middle Ages the concept of natural law became further refined. Among its primary proponents included Peter Abelard (1079–1142) and the greatest theologian of the era, Thomas Aquinas (ca. 1225–1274). Most of the Medieval Scholastics were especially indebted to the vision of the world as a living being articulated by Plato in his treatise *Timaeus*.[12]

Of course there were more ancient precedents of the concept in Christianity. Writing sometime between AD 54 and 58, the Apostle Paul wrote:

> When Gentiles, who do not possess the law, do instinctively what the law requires, these, though not having the law, are a law to themselves. They show that what the law requires is written on their hearts, to which their own conscience bears witness. (Romans 2:14–15)

The idea that all people intuitively know the contents of the Mosaic law is clearly rooted in the New Testament.

With the Middle Ages and the beginning of the modern era, the concept of the natural law became increasingly influential on Western politics. By the seventeenth century, at least in England, the natural law had become the basis of established legal standard. But it was only applied to nations and their kings, on grounds that they alone were in a true state of nature, not governed by some sovereign.[13] At the end of the century, two Enlightenment philosophers who had important impact on America's Founders, John Locke (1632–1704) and Thomas Reid (1710–1796), along with his school of Scottish Common Sense Realism, were basing their philosophy and politics on the concept of natural law, applying it broadly to all realms of human behavior. Locke spoke of certain "natural rights" and how the law of nature should decide all controversies. Some interpreters have suggested that this equation of natural law with rights represented a change in the content of the natural law, but as we shall subsequently demonstrate, that will not be substantiated.[14] Likewise, Reid's references to all human beings having a moral common sense, and also at points referring to natural rights, represented a modification of, but no formal divergence from, the older view.[15] This revised concept of the natural law was very much in the air that America's Founders breathed.

An Ethic for All Americans

I have focused on the Christian concept of the natural law, because it was largely though this tradition that the concept was appropriated by the American Constitutional system. But in no sense should this be construed as entailing that only in Christianity do we find such a concept. As we noted it is not foreign to the other great monotheisms found in America.

Clearly something like a concept of the natural law is evident in the rabbinic literature of Judaism. Thus, Yalkut Shimoni to Prophets (296) is recorded as stating that all know the difference between right and wrong, and can practice righteousness. In the Islamic heritage, there is a passage in the Koran (7:172–173) that states that all the children of Adam are aware of Allah, and so all are justly accountable to the divine judgment. Like Christians, Muslims believe that all have an intuitive awareness of the Will of God.

It is clearly apparent, that that concept of the natural law is not an idea that is peculiar to Christianity. Even the Secularist has ownership of this notion, not just in view of the concept's affirmation that all people share common values of good—and in view of the affirmation of the contents of the last five or six of the Ten Commandments in the legal statutes of most Western nations (a point we need to verify in a moment)—but also in view of the latest cutting-edge research in genetic biology.

Edward O. Wilson is a biologist who developed the theory of socio-biology. According to this theory's basic tenets, genetic evolution has brought humans to the point where they are dependent on culture in order to flourish and survive. The learned behaviors and enforced cooperation culture makes possible are in the interest of human genes, because humans intuitively know their genes will be proliferated maximally through such cooperation. And society or culture enforces altruism, behavior that increases the fitness of the other, even if it is at one's own expense.[16] Insofar as the Ten Commandments pertaining to our responsibility toward our fellow human beings teach this sort of altruism, in essence Wilson seems to imply a kind of natural law with his observations.

The concept of natural law is obviously a most inclusive one. But for our purposes, the most impressive statement of the inclusiveness of the concept for all Americans, that it is a way of doing politics and ethics that excludes no one, is evident in the prominence of the concept in the founding American documents.

The American Constitutional System and the Natural Law

For the Founders, the aim of government was not to establish Christian values or love in society, but justice. And justice is not a function of the teachings and actions of Jesus recorded in the Gospel, but is a function of law, the natural law. Writing in *The Federalist Papers*, a series of publications written to support ratification of the Constitution while the Articles of Confederation were still in effect, James Madison asserted:

> Justice is the end of government. It is the end of civil society.[17]

The natural law is certainly an aspect of the American political system, from the Declaration of Independence's appeal to the "self-evident" truths, to numerous appeals to the concept in order to authorize our Constitutional system in *The Federalist Papers*. In a number of these cases, such appeals take the form of invoking "common sense" and "good sense"—evidences of the Founders' reliance on the Common Sense Realist philosophy of Thomas Reid.[18] In these same documents, Madison appeals to the concept of natural law, "which declares that the safety and happiness of society are the objects at which all political institutions aim," in order to justify overriding the Articles of Confederation. Alexander Hamilton makes such an appeal viewing the natural law as the norm for judicial decisions involving conflicting laws.[19]

There is even some suggestion of an appeal to this concept in Jefferson's famed 1802 Letter referring to the "wall of separation between church and State," as he states that "no natural right [is] in opposition to his [humanity's] social duties.[20] This argument makes it evident that in the Founders' minds (at least in Jefferson's view) appeals to the natural law are in no sense a violation of the separation of church and state. There need be no compunction about the Democrats or the Republicans appealing to the natural law in order to authorize policies. It is an unambiguously inclusive concept.

But Can the Natural Law Help You Get Elected Today?

In view of the case we have made in previous chapters for the importance of the Puritan Paradigm in understanding American society and in explaining the conservative Republican hegemony, it is logical to wonder whether the natural law might be a barrier to electability today. The argument I have mounted for recommending to Democrats and their friends in the religious community that religion be injected into policy rhetoric and deliberations by appealing only to the natural law, not to distinct Christian teachings of the Church's interpretation of Jesus, is in contrast to characteristically Puritan ways of thinking. Recall that a core supposition of Puritanism has been that we should take our bearings in social polity from the teachings of Jesus and His Gospel. In fact, though, that is not the whole story.

It was previously pointed out that the natural law has been part of the Puritan heritage from its inception. In these earlier chapters I noted the role of *The Westminster Confession of Faith* as Puritanism's foundational theological document. At one point in this Confession (Art.XXIII.7), the natural law is taught. The roots for this affirmation are even older. Recall that Puritanism is itself the spiritual daughter of the thought of John Calvin, and he also taught the natural law at some points in his career.[21]

On the American scene, it is interesting to note that one of the prime representatives of the Puritan heritage at the time of American Revolution, Presbyterian pastor and president of its college at Princeton, New Jersey, John Witherspoon, also affirmed the natural law. Like his mentor Thomas Reid, to whose Common Sense Realist philosophy he was so indebted, Witherspoon affirmed that all human beings possess a common moral sense.[22] It is evident, then, that appeals to the natural law for your politics are not necessarily antithetical to the spirit of Puritanism. Democrats and their friends in the religious community would do well to educate the public regarding the Biblical roots of this doctrine, how most American religious bodies (even those that are part of the Puritan Paradigm) affirm it. Of course, without patient explanation, political appeals to the natural law may be perceived by those on the Right as "un-Christian" or irreligious. But at least such an argument does not flirt with the First Amendment compromises we have seen may be implied by wholehearted endorsement of the Puritan proposal to have public policy directed by distinct Christian principles. In addition, appealing to the natural law need not alienate the elite New Democrats' secular base, like the characteristic Puritan orientation of Bush and his buddies does.

Making this distinction between the natural law and distinct Christian teachings clearly may help the Democrats affect broader coalitions in other ways in 2008. As long as Christian teachings are thought directly to impact politics, some conservatives might associate women's subordination with their faith commitments, and then in turn find voting for Hillary Clinton or some other qualified woman Presidential candidate problematic. But if it is clear to these Christians that politics is normed by the natural law, it might be easier on those grounds to argue that a woman's eligibility to hold our highest political office is just a matter of justice (a rendering to Caesar [Mark 12:16–17]).

No one should conclude that I think that my points about the consistency of appeals to the natural law with Puritan thinking matter to the electorate as a whole. In some ways, my argument for the consistency of appeals to the natural law with Puritan thinking is mounted only for experts and readers like yourself. American voters do not self-consciously care if politicians embody Puritan values. But at least a significant number of them care about having their religious values represented in politics. They care if "Christian values" are reflected in our politics (almost seven of ten Americans, according to a July 2005 poll).[23] And recall that for most of them, Christianity tends to be subliminally understood in accord with Puritan thinking. In any case, it will be sufficient for Democrats to point out to religious people (especially Christians) the Biblical basis for the natural law, as we noted earlier in Romans 2:14–15.

What the Natural Law Teaches: Political Implications

Of course most religiously oriented readers already know the contents of the natural law, by virtue of their having been taught the Ten Commandments. They know that it is wrong to reject the authority of parents and superiors, to kill, steal, commit adultery, lie, and covet. This is pretty much common sense for all of us.

In response to previously cited critics who contend that the distinctively religious character of the concept of natural law has been supplanted with a preoccupation with human rights since the Enlightenment, so that references to the natural law in the Constitutional system are bereft of religious significance as I have been suggesting, the eminent Williams College historian Francis Oakley has demonstrated that in the evolution of the concept there is no clear indication that the concept's content has changed.[24]

Indeed, there are some indications that the Founders and the main influences on their thought understood the natural law not just in terms of individual rights, but linked these rights seamlessly to the standards very much in harmony with those commandments of the Judeo-Christian Decalogue that pertain to our responsibilities to our fellow human beings. Writing in his *Second Treatise on Civil Government*, John Locke not only affirmed human equality, but then proceeded to assert:

> The state of nature has a law of nature to govern it, which obliges every one, and reason, which is that law, teaches all mankind, who will but consult it, that being all equal and independent, no one ought to harm another in this life, health, liberty, or possessions.[25]

This certainly sounds like the Ten Commandments' strictures against murder and theft. Likewise Thomas Reid stated that the obligations of moral common sense may be summarized as "the love of God and the love of our neighbor."[26]

On the American Continent itself, Benjamin Franklin spoke of twelve commandments, adding the commandments to increase and replenish the earth as well as to love one another. These were more important, he claims, than the other ten.[27] Franklin's observation is not inconsistent with an affirmation that the content of the natural law accords with what the great monotheisms of America claim to be the last half of the Ten Commandments (the so-called Second Table). All laws are to be in harmony with these common sense intuitive ethical norms. And no law should be passed that contradicts these norms.

Sometimes when people think about the Ten Commandments, they tend only to dwell on the negative—on the "Thou shall nots." Such thinking led less informed political pundits like Bill Press incorrectly to conclude that the Ten Commandments have little to do with American jurisprudence.[28] However, his views incorrectly overlook how the Christian community in Western society has interpreted the Commandments and the impact this transdenominational interpretation has had on jurisprudence and legislative strategies. For in fact there is a long history in Christian communities of understanding these Commandments to have positive significance, to connote things we should do, not just to forbid certain behaviors. Clarifying these transdenominational interpretations not only offers hard evidence regarding how significant American legislation embodies the values of the Second Table of the Ten Commandments. Such an analysis also suggests some progressive public policy proposals.

How the Church's Interpretations of the Natural Law Can and Already Have Guided Domestic Legislation

In view of the fact that Christians contend that the natural law may be understood by reason or intuition common to all, and is not a function of faith, it is also appropriate to draw on some of the interpretations of the Ten Commandments (which is the content of the natural law) taught by various Christian denominations. As I already suggested, many of these seem to authorize the Democratic agenda, which further demonstrates that these interpretations have an inclusive character. Nevertheless, an occasional reference to these documents by Democrats, at least in certain contexts, would further emphasize their openness to the voice of religion in the public square—would be one more indication that they had "gotten religion."

It is intriguing that for all the talk of relativism and the lament that we have lost common values in America, the standard interpretations of the Ten Commandments by several denominations have a remarkable similarity. To be sure, Catholics and some Protestants may disagree on the meaning of the Commandment "Thou shall not kill" with regard to abortion and stem-cell research. However, such lack of unanimity on the meaning of the Commandments and their political implications is the exception, not the rule.

For instance, to take my own Lutheran commitments as a starting point, in his *Small Catechism*, which Martin Luther wrote for the purpose of educating the young in the faith (a document that still remains authoritative for Lutherans), the Reformer explains the Commandment "Thou shall not kill" as follows:

> We are to fear and love God, so that we neither endanger nor harm the lives of our neighbors, but instead to help and support them in all of life's needs.[29]

The official interpretation of this commandment for Lutherans mandates outreach to the poor and providing support for their needs. Failure to do so by individuals and governments is to be a murderer. Presbyterians and the United Church of Christ heritage agree. In their *Larger Catechism*, a document rooted in seventeenth-century Puritanism, this Commandment is said to mean that we are to be about comforting and succoring the distressed.[30] These interpretations seem to favor the creation of government safety nets for the poor, practices instituted in the sixteenth century by both Martin Luther and John Calvin.

Similar points are made by these traditions along with the Roman Catholic and Methodist heritages in their mutual interpretations of the Commandment against theft. Collectively all of them take positions at least somewhat critical of the unbridled free market.

Again writing in his *Small Catechism* (and echoing 1 John 3:17), Martin Luther states:

> We are to fear and love God, so that we neither take our neighbors' money or property nor acquire them by using shoddy merchandise or crooked deals, but instead help them to improve and protect their property and income.[31]

The first Reformer elaborated further on this point in *The Large Catechism* as he lamented how daily "the poor are defrauded" in the free market, as "new burdens and higher prices are imposed." He then proceeds to warn about how we deal with the poor who must live from hand to mouth.[32] There is a clear suggestion here of the Reformer's own practice of establishing economic safety nets for the poor in cities where Lutherans dominated. Getting religion helps the Democrats on these points.

Though predictably not as overtly critical of the free market, Presbyterians likewise claim in their authoritative Puritan document *The Larger Catechism* that we are "by all just and lawful means to procure, preserve, and further the wealth and outward estate of others, as well as our own." Even in the Methodist heritage, we can identify John Wesley explicating this commandment with a warning against trying to make profitable deals at our neighbors' expense. Likewise in the official, papal-sponsored *Catechism of the Catholic Church*, citing a famous preacher of the Church's first centuries, the bishops state:

> "Not to enable the poor to share in our goods is to steal from them and deprive them of life. The good we possess are not ours, but theirs." "The demands of justice must be satisfied first of all, that which is already due in justice is not to be offered as a gift of charity. . . ." Hence, those who are oppressed by poverty are the object of a *preferential love*.[33]

Showing preference to the poor, using all lawful means to further the wealth of others, is in line with old Democratic Party thinking — the Party of Roosevelt, Kennedy, and Johnson. These texts might even be used as allies in mounting arguments today for Affirmative Action, as well as debt relief and international aid for developing nations in the Southern Hemisphere. Dialogue with religious traditions, especially their concept of the natural law, can be good for Democrats, good for America.

Of course it is imperative that those invoking these interpretations of the Decalogue make it clear for the public that the denominational teachings advocated are not distinctively Christian, that they are common sense insights drawn from reason and the concept of social justice (the natural law). This point will need to be made emphatically in order to ensure that the secular, Jewish, and growing Muslim bases of the Party are not turned off in the bid to broaden the constituency by appealing to Christian voters.

Democrats would be politically savvy to draw on these observations from the denominations we have been considering. It would put to rest the sense that they are not speaking about values, not concerned about the input of religion. At the very least, such appeals might be attractive to the often-forgotten membership of these denominations, and it would force Republican members of these denominations to consider how their own political preferences might not be as in accord with their belief systems as they think. Religious leaders of these denominations who are inclined to progressive politics might make these teachings better known to their communities. Such teaching would have immediate Christian education value and might just make some political difference.

The stated concern for the poor and those without power, which we have identified in the mainline Protestant and Catholic bodies just described, also reflects expressly in the American Constitution. For its commitments to the separation of powers (the three branches of government) emerge from the recognition that there is de facto a kind of class warfare that will inevitably emerge in American politics whenever people organize themselves into societies. In fact, the language used by the Founders to interpret this Constitutional commitment closely parallels the Christian doctrine of Original Sin. This is the other doctrine that will be good to emphasize by those who want a politics of the Left that can challenge the present Republican hegemony. Taking seriously the doctrine of Original Sin makes our politics more real.

THE AUGUSTINIAN VIEW OF ORIGINAL SIN

We have already noted the presence of this Christian commitment in the American Constitutional system. But because of the optimistic view of human nature associated with much Republican laissez-faire politics (an optimism inherited from both Revivalist roots and the modern infatuation with relativism), as well as the diminution of this doctrine in the mainline denominations as a result of the previously described impact of Enlightenment thinking on them, it is necessary to begin with the exposition of precisely what convictions are entailed by a traditional Christian understanding of Original Sin.

Without such clarification we will be plagued by misunderstandings. For most Americans, indeed most Christians worldwide, think of Sin in terms of misdeeds. In fact, Original Sin refers to a state. It posits that since the Fall into Sin (depicted in Genesis 3) human beings are essentially selfish or "concupiscent."

The doctrine of Original Sin and its correlated view of human nature was developed by the great third–fourth century North African theologian and philosopher, St. Augustine. He was not the first to describe Sin as a fallen state. But it was his writings that led the Church eventually to embrace the doctrine.[34]

In order to make clear that human beings are totally dependent on the grace of God with regard to salvation and anything they can accomplish, Augustine referred to our bondage to Sin. Such bondage to Sin does not necessarily mean that we are reduced to robots. It is theologically appropriate on his grounds to continue to assert our freedom to choose actions without compromising the claim that we are in bondage to Sin. For example, it might be possible to assert that you have a choice about whether to cease your present activity of reading in order to rest or sleep. On Augustine's grounds, either way you are sinning, because the decision you make in either case is self-serving (doing what makes you feel good).[35]

The challenge next faced by Augustine was how unequivocally to assert our bondage to Sin. The weight of precedent and how the Biblical witness had been interpreted in previous centuries moved him to talk about Sin as something we are born with and to depict it in terms of desire or lust.[36] When we are lusting (be it sexual or lust for power or things), we are in bondage to that person or thing. You cannot make many free decisions in the heat of passion. You just do what the lust demands.

Augustine described this bondage to lust as *concupiscence*, designating such lusts as the "law of sin."[37] Of course concupiscence is a term that refers to a strong, compelling desire, especially sexual lust. The term had autobiographical significance for the African Father insofar as he had struggled with sexual lust in the course of his spiritual pilgrimage. By employing the term to describe the essence of Sin, he provided a powerful way of expressing the bondage without reducing fallen humanity to mere robots. Just as in the heat of sexual passion we cannot stop the sexual encounter, so sinners seeking their own gratification cannot stop seeking, even when they know better.

Augustine's views seem confirmed by St. Paul's writings in Romans 7:15, 19: "I do not understand my own actions. For I do not do what I want, but I do the very thing I hate. . . . For I do not do the good I want, but the evil I do not want is what I do." Augustine conceives of fallen human beings as addicts. Like addicts, the more we are driven to seek pleasure and fulfillment, the less we will be satisfied, and so the more we will seek. The more you desire, the more you sin, and the more you sin, the more you desire.[38]

It would be a mistake to understand Augustine to be defining Sin merely as lustful actions that result in visible violations of the Ten Commandments. His point in describing Sin as concupiscence was to make clear that *all* human deeds, even the ones outwardly good, are sinful. Augustine did believe sinful human beings are capable of outwardly good deeds. Indeed, such acts are no less outwardly good than deeds motivated by the love of God.[39] There is a sense, on Augustine's grounds, that the behavior of Abraham Lincoln and Martin Luther King Jr. was not better than that of the likes of Hitler and Osama bin Laden. All were driven in some sense by lust for power and influence (concupiscence).

At least some of these insights are consistent with modern biological insights. Biochemists have increasingly demonstrated that love may be related to the chemicals the body secretes when members of the opposite sex are attracted to each other. In the early stages of the relationship, each partner is flooded with chemical cousins of amphetamines, notably the chemical phenylethylamine. Like any amphetamine, the body builds up a tolerance to this chemical, explaining why passionate love cools. But in long-term relations a new chemical, oxytocin, is secreted. This chemical produces different kinds of pleasurable reactions, like the desire to snuggle or a sense of security and calm.[40]

Science has here confirmed what Augustine knew all along. The very best of human activities, even love, is selfish. We love because it feels good. The Christian doctrine of Original Sin as first articulated by St. Augustine makes good sense scientifically. It also makes good sense politically, both from the standpoint of the American Constitution, but also makes sense realistically in terms of the hardball politics it takes to bring about good public policy. The Founders anticipated it would be that way.

Original Sin in the Constitution

There are numerous examples of America's Founders maintaining Augustinian convictions about human nature. Among those who affirmed this view included James Madison, Gouverneur Morris (who warned against the rich seeking to establish dominion over everyone else), Alexander Hamilton (who claimed that "men love power"), and Benjamin Franklin (who reminded delegates to the Constitutional Convention that men are driven by "ambition and avarice").[41] Franklin made a similar point interpreting virtues in an Augustinian sense, as a kind of concupiscence. He wrote: "Almost every Man has a strong Desire of being valu'd and esteem'd by the rest of his Species."[42]

In two of his famed contributions to *The Federalist Papers*, Madison generalized these Augustinian observations, applying them to groups (factions) that emerge in any free society.[43] These factions, he contended, always aim to establish their own self-interest at the expense of everyone else. The idea of "class warfare" is not the creation of Karl Marx. It is a Constitutional idea. Madison's *Preface to Debates in the Convention* also refers to "weakness and wants of man naturally leading to an association of individuals" and to "feeble communities" resorting to a Union.[44] The core rationale for forming governments is self-interest or selfishness.

Another way in which we find an Augustinian vision of human nature in Madison's thought is in his appreciation of the herd mentality of the public. This was a crucial supposition for his contention that we need government structures to protect us from the tyranny of the mob. He wrote:

> If it be true that all governments rest on opinion, it is no less true that the strength of opinion in each individual, and its practical influence on his conduct depend much on the number which he supposes to have entertained the same opinion. The reason of man, like man himself, is timid and cautious when left alone, and acquires firmness and confidence in proportion to the number which it is associated.[45]

Just because the majority favors a policy does not mean it is in the best interests of the nation or even the best interests of the majority itself. In fact, we are creatures quite likely to be swayed by the crowd, to go along with what most people are saying even if we really don't agree with them. The Madisonian observation certainly explains clothing fashions, and why they frequently change. But he warns us to apply these insights to understanding politics. It is good that the United States is not a pure democracy.

In one of the other of *The Federalist Papers* Madison proceeded to explain how and why the majority is likely to victimize minorities:

> Different interests necessarily exist in different classes of citizens. If a majority be united by a common interest, the rights of the minority will be insecure.[46]

It is evident why we need big government, why "states' rights" can lead to vicitimization of the poor and oppressed. Is it also not the case that we need to be careful when the majority favors laissez-faire economics and globalization? The small nation and the factory worker are likely to become victims.

Elsewhere Madison also appealed to an Augustinian-like view of human nature in order to explain the oppressive predispositions of majorities:

> there are particular moments in public affairs when the people, stimulated by some irregular passion, or some illicit advantage, or misled by the artful representations of interested men, may call for measures which they themselves will afterwards be the most ready to lament and condemn.[47]

In these affirmations Madison was following the Calvinist teachings of his great teacher John Witherspoon. In fact, in a speech made to the Continental Congress as the Articles of Confederation were being drafted, Witherspoon asserted: "I am none of those who either deny or conceal the depravity of human nature."[48]

It is evident that if the Democrats were to embrace the Augustinian version of the doctrine of Original Sin, they would not only "get religion," in a Christian sense. They, rather than the Republicans, would be the Party most in touch with the core suppositions of the Constitution.

Structural Implications of Original Sin

Given this pessimistic, realistic view of human nature, the Founders then shared with Augustine a realistic view of government and its coercive function. Alexander Hamilton writes:

> Why has government been instituted at all? Because the passions of men will not conform to the dictates of reason and justice without constraint.[49]

The Founders believed that America's size and diversity would protect the new nation from the self-love that leads to factions. Madison writes:

> In the extended republic of the United States, and among the great variety of interests, parties, and sects which it embraces, a coalition of the majority of the whole society could seldom take place on any other principles than those of justice and the general good.[50]

Given the concupiscent, self-interested character of human nature, we need the coercion affected by government and our peers in order to make us tolerable and to recognize what really is good. But we are so self-centered that we need government to make us do the good despite ourselves. Are government regulations, of the sort that the Democrats have historically advocated, really as unconstitutional as the Right contends? The next time Bush and his Republican coalition lament or try to peel back government regulations in the name of maintaining the freedom of the majority, or debunk suspicions about their upper-class interests at the expense of the poor, the Democrats just need to "get religion" and invoke the Constitution's view of human nature, its separation of powers, and its supposition that class (factional) warfare is inevitable. Granted, this is religion more harmonious with the Christian vision. But while not teaching Original Sin, both Judaism (2 Samuel 11; Amos 2:6–7; Jonah 1:3; 4:1–4; Job 31; 32:2) and Islam (Koran 30:29) are open to talking about human selfishness. After all, it is part of the Constitutional vision.

Of course we are well aware of how this view of human beings led the Founders to opt for the separation of powers in the three branches of government. Perhaps less well known is how the idea emerged in harmony with the Augustinian theological supposition we have been considering. It is interesting that long before the Constitutional Convention (or the Revolution for that matter), Madison's Presbyterian teacher Witherspoon was expounding such a vision. In a 1772 treatise this mentor of Madison wrote:

> Every good form of government must be complex . . . so that one Principle may check the other. . . . It is folly to expect that a state should be upheld by integrity of all who have a share in managing it. They must be so balanced that when one draws his own interest or inclination, there may be an over poise upon the whole.[51]

The American nation's political system is at least to some extent clearly a reflection of the Christian vision of human nature. Democrats will do well to get that word out. It will help all of us to take into account the realities of American politics. It reminds us that concupiscent people will always ask what is in it for them. Consequently, horse-trading is part of the game, and the politician always has to ask how the position taken will play with the voters. The Left and its religiously inclined friends need to get real about politics.

We have already referred to another benefit of this view of Sin applied to politics, that the doctrine represents a critique of the Bush coalition and the Religious Right's optimistic view of human nature, which underlies the advocacy of laissez-faire economics. But recognizing that this view of human nature is embedded in the American political system seems to entail that we should be able to identify a critical perspective on laissez-faire economics in the Founders' thinking. In fact, we can identify several overlooked suggestions by the Founders, based on their realism about human nature, which is most suggestive of managed economics of the New Deal and Great Society programs.

The Founders on Economics and Poverty

Much to the surprise of interested observers, since the finding conflicts with commonly accepted truisims, the primary leader among the Founders' generation on economics, Alexander Hamilton, clearly took a position at odds with Adam Smith and his free-market convictions. In his "Report on Manufactures," the Founder wrote:

> Experience teaches that men are often so much governed by what they are accustomed to see and practice, that the simplest and most obvious improvements, in the [most] ordinary occupations, are adopted with hesitation, reluctance and by slow gradations.[52]

Hamilton's observation may further help explain points made by Thomas Frank in his recent best seller, *What's the Matter with Kansas?* regarding how many Americans have been voting enthusiastically for Bush and his policies, even though it is against their own economic interests.[53]

Such convictions even seem to reflect in the Constitution's views regarding income and property distribution. John Locke, whose concepts clearly influenced America's Founders, to some extent held a view of property and government's role in its redistribution much like Madison and his colleagues were later to endorse. The natural law demands equity. About the matter he wrote:

> The same law of nature that does by this means give us property does also bound that property too. . . . But how far has he [God] given it us, *to enjoy*? As much as any one can make use of to any advantage of life before it spoils, so much he may by his labour for a property in. Whatever is beyond this is more than his share, and belongs to others.[54]

Thomas Jefferson also seems to have been no champion of the unbridled free market. He and his colleagues in the Commonwealth of Virginia opted for setting a maximum 5 percent interest rates on loans.[55] In fact, writing earlier in a correspondence with James Madison, he stated a case for the redistribution of property among the poor:

> I am conscious that an equal division of property is impracticable, but the consequences of this enormous inequality producing so much misery to the bulk of mankind, legislators cannot invent too many devices for subdividing property, only taking care to let the subdivisions go hand in hand with the natural affectations of the human mind. . . . [W]henever there are in any country uncultivated lands and unemployed poor, it is clear that the laws of property have been so far extended as to violate natural right. . . . If for the encouragement of industry we allow it [the land] to be appropriated, we must take care that other employment be provided to those excluded from appropriation.[56]

If not providing authorization for the development of modern welfare programs, the Founders' commitment to the regulation of the market, including creation of jobs through public works projects, is certainly in line with modern Democratic policies. Other Founders opting for similar policies include Benjamin Franklin, Alexander Hamilton, and James Madison. Remarks by all three, in that order, follow:

> All Property, indeed except the Savage's temporary Cabin, his Bow, his Matchcoat . . . seems to me to be the Creature of public Convention. Hence the Public has the Right of Regulating Descents, and all other Conveyances of Property and even of limiting the Quantity and Uses of it. All the Property that is necessary to a Man, for the Conservation of the Individual and

Propagation of the Species, is his natural Right, which none can justly deprive him of: But all Property superfluous to such purposes is the Property of the Publick . . . who may therefore by other Laws dispose of it, whenever the Welfare of the Publick shall demand such Disposition.[57]

Happy it is when the interest which the government has in the preservation of its own power coincides with a proper distribution of the public burdens and trend to guard the least wealthy part of the community from oppression.[58]

[T]he great objection should be to combat the evil [of faction] by withholding *unnecessary* opportunities from a few. . . . By the silent operation of laws, which without violating the rights of property reduce extreme wealth towards a state of mediocrity, and raise extreme indigence towards a state of comfort.[59]

This sort of commitment to government's role in managing the economy had roots in America's Colonial era. The Pilgrims themselves in Massachusetts undertook legal proceedings against those who sought to get the full amount the market would yield for their goods, business practices that were deemed greedy.[60] Democratic economic policies to protect consumers and the poor from exploitation can claim Constitutional and even Puritan roots. Democrats and their friends need to get that word out.

CONCLUDING REFLECTIONS: HOW TAKING SIN AND THE NATURAL LAW INTO ACCOUNT HELPS DEMOCRATS, AND THE RISKS INVOLVED

An awareness of the sinful character of human nature, of the fact that we will always be concupiscent, seeking to achieve our own aims in everything we do, entails that you and I are not trustworthy. I have already pointed out how when you see human beings in this way, more government regulations are desirable, in order to keep our self-seeking efforts in check. Once again it is evident that a little bit of religion (in this case, an affirmation of the Christian doctrine of Original Sin) is good for Democrats. I hasten to add, though, that this point runs both ways. Even governmental structures and the people who administer them are not free of concupiscence. Consequently big government, without the threat and supervision of the people, easily becomes tyrannical. Getting serious about Original Sin, shedding some of the optimism that has characterized Republican free-market mania and American society in general in recent decades, can be good for Republicans and good for America too.

We have considered two ways (not just affirmation of the doctrine of Original Sin, but also an affirmation of the concept of the natural law) in which Democrats could "get religion" in noncontroversial, common-sense ways. These are ways, quite obviously, that would not need to offend Constitutional sensibilities, to the benefit of Democrats' image. Of course, there could be resistance to affirming the Christian view of Original Sin in some Democratic circles. It not only goes against the grain of Republican optimism about what human beings can accomplish when unhindered. It also represents a critique of today's naive optimism about human nature, about what we can accomplish as the accompanying therapeutic rhetoric about the mad chase for self-fulfillment and the importance of having "our needs met" and "being good to ourselves." But these modes of life have not been good for America, as our present cultural ennui, greed, and declining standards testify. No doubt about it. The Christian view of Original Sin, coupled with an affirmation of the natural law, is the kind of religion that is good for America, something that can help get us back to our Constitutional moorings. Although the spiritual psyche of many Americans has been saturated by the optimism and relativistic "do your own thing" ethos of the media and the academy, the view of Original Sin (and even to a lesser extent the appeal to the natural law) we have been describing will also have a certain resonance insofar as it taps into one of the core elements of the Puritan Paradigm (the total depravity of human nature).[61]

These observations give us a little taste of why getting the right kind of religion can be good for the Democrats and good for America. But how to implement this? What do Christians and their churches need to do? What are the best ways for Democratic consultants to talk about religion and politics? That is what we need to consider in the closing chapter.

10

What Catholics and Protestants Will Need to Do to Keep Jesus and His Gospel from Becoming Conservative: Some New (Old) Alternatives

We have been noting in the last several chapters how the classical Christian doctrines and their implications for contemporary sociopolitical life have been muted by a combination of prevailing social trends and the dominant theological models of our day. When you individualize the Gospel with a therapeutic bias, when you approach the Bible consistently with a critical and relativistic mind-set regarding truth, what you are left with is a version of Christianity that does not stand over and against your own best interests. In fact, this version of Christianity gives us permission to see its "authentic" mandates as being virtually identical with whatever the cultural gurus attest to be the latest trends for a healthy, happy, fulfilling life. Oftentimes, the Bible does not mean what it literally says, proponents of this dominant theological model contend. We need to look for connections between its spirit (what the Disciples intended to communicate in their primitive categories and stories) and our present way of life. More often than not, the media and business have convinced large segments of the American public that it really wants self-fulfillment, material possessions, and the freedom from constraint that comes with economic prosperity.

Of course we may not really be sure we want these things, but the media and the crowd tell us we do. And so do many of our churches, because their theological leaders have bought into this view or the style of thinking that makes it possible. In view of the unhappiness and ennui in many pockets of America, in view of the shrinking standard of living (we only rank eighth internationally on that score), and in view of the growing gap between the rich and the poor, the growth of poverty in post-Reagan America, what can we do about it?

137

As we have seen, if mainline American Protestant Christianity and American Catholicism are going to make a difference—to stop being the religious advocate of the Republican sanctification of the free market at the expense of the poor and the middle class—they need to learn some lessons from the Religious Right. These large denominations need to break with the models of theology that have been prevailing in their seminaries at least since World War II and embrace a more conservative approach to Biblical studies, even affirming the literal meaning of those Biblical texts that seem to resemble a narrative or a letter. It will take that kind of theology in order for the majority of the public, influenced as it is by Puritan ways of thinking and its belief in the divine inspiration of the Bible, to seriously consider a Jesus Who is not conservative. The continuing liberal political agenda of those bodies we noted in chapters 5 and 6 will not resonate with the American public. They will be perceived as non-Christian by the majority of the American public if they continue to couch these proposals in the categories of multiculturalism, relativism, and therapy, and not in terms of the literal sense of the Bible. Keep in mind that according to a November 2004 Gallup poll, 82 percent of the public believe the Bible is inspired and should be taken literally at least sometimes. (One-third of the public would have it read literally in all situations, and only 15 percent regard it as legends and moral precepts.) It is evident again: The theology that has prevailed in American seminaries and undergraduate religion departments at least since World War II, if not before, needs to be revisited.

For the sake of argument, let's suppose religiously inclined Democrats and theological allies in the mainline churches formed an alliance much like Republicans and the Right. Let us also suppose that this coalition was able to retain the socially liberal, unchurched elements of the present Democratic establishment. And let's further suppose that this coalition even took my advice, breaking with the Puritan Paradigm's commitment to trying to impose Christian values on society and instead formulated their liberal policies by appealing to the natural law for authorization and the Constitutional precedents for not trusting the majority or the unregulated free market. That sort of approach, as we saw in the last chapter, would be the religious Democrats' best strategy for maintaining the coalition with socially liberal, unchurched elements of the Party. But if the spokespersons of this coalition remained wedded to the academy's favorite trends of late, like DeConstruction and relativism, the public as a whole would not hear these politically progressive proposals as compatible with their faith. For such a theological proposal would likely be heard as not believing in absolute truth, as well as being too critical in its approach to Scripture. And given the Puritan suppositions of most Americans, which as we have seen tilts them toward a free-market, individualistic orientation (the heritage of Puritanism and modern Revivalism), the policies of this new liberal coalition would be regarded as secularist, as not embodying Christian values. Let's try to understand why, in a bit more detail.

A presentation of some liberal, pro-labor policy, on grounds that a critical approach to the forms of labor and the relationship between rich and poor advocated by the Church as depicted in the Bible must be undertaken, leads a theologically conservative public to conclude that the proposal has no valid Biblical basis. It goes against the prevailing pro–free-market Puritan readings of the Bible.

The same dynamic will transpire if the pro-labor policy is advocated on grounds of explicating the natural law regarding the Commandment concerning theft though the eyes of the poor. A theologically conservative public is likely to deem such an interpretation of the natural law as arbitrary, as just the opinion of certain elite leaders of the mainline denominations.

In previous chapters we have noted how, since the Enlightenment, Western society has bought into a relativism. Most of us, save those belonging to the Religious Right or the denizens of some rural enclaves without many college graduates, believe that truth is not objective or that everyone's version of the truth is equally valid. Consequently, there is nothing really new about any theological-political proposal trading on these suppositions. And since political liberalism calls for some sacrifice by the bourgeoisie on behalf of the poor, as well as certain limits on our freedom that big government and its regulations impose on us, when it comes to an arbitrary choice between political liberalism and conservatism the conservative position will win all the time among the privileged.

It would be different, though, if mainline churches got over their critical mind-set and relativism when it comes to the way the Bible and experience are interpreted. A faith perspective that can lay claim to descriptive or consensus understanding of the Word of God has an authority that it does not have if it is just the version of some segment of the faithful. The claim to descriptive meaning is also counter-cultural, going against the grain of what the leadership of most of the elite churches and the cultural gurus of contemporary America deem possible. And counter-cultural movements sometimes command the attention of the American public and its media in ways that mainstream institutions do not.

This has been the problem for the mainline churches in America since the church-growth explosion at the end of the 1950s, if not earlier. The larger Protestant bodies, and even the Catholic Church since the Second Vatican Council and the election of John Kennedy, have come to be seen as embodying establishment values and lifestyles. (Of course, to have the American churches be seen as embodying establishment values was nothing new, just a continuation of the heritage of Puritanism and its commitment to the Church's role in shaping societal norms.) What was new, besides the incorporation of non-Puritan religious bodies such as Catholicism into this Paradigm, was that cultural change beginning in the 1960s made this vision of the relation between Christianity and the American establishment problematic. For, since the 1960s through the present decade, American society has become more secularized. Social life, entertainment, and education are no longer governed by Christian values, principles, or ways of thinking. Bible stories, the ideal of the single lifelong marriage, character, and even justice for the oppressed do not count nearly as much as hooking up, being good to yourself, flexibility, women's liberation, making money, DeConstruction, and rapping about all them "hos." The old Protestant establishment and the increasingly Americanized Catholic Church are perceived today by the media and academic elite as embodying values of a bygone era.

Of course, as we have already noted, these denominations have tried to make themselves relevant. At least in their seminaries, and even in the denominational headquarters, they have tried to appropriate cutting-edge social trends—a politically liberal, progressive posture and contemporary music in worship in the 1960s, critical approaches to the Bible and its authority even earlier, psychotherapy and Feminism in the 1970s, and gay marriages and the Ordination of practicing homosexuals, along with computer literacy, DeConstruction, and the business-management techniques of running congregations today.

Unfortunately, though, the mainline churches have never been at the forefront of these trends, always playing catch-up to the media, the intelligentsia, or even to the Religious Right. Besides, the majority of the membership of these churches has not bought into these developments anyway. The ordinary mainline churchgoers are still too conservative for most of these trends. Little wonder, then, that these denominations have become so culturally and politically irrelevant. Church leaders can take all the progressive social and ethical positions, but the media and the politicians know that they cannot deliver any votes for these causes from their constituents.

Conservative about ecclesiastical and worldview matters as they are (we have already noted how 82 percent of the American public believes in taking the Bible literally, at least sometimes, and nearly half the public rejects the Theory of Evolution), most members of these mainline churches and even parish pastors turned off by the perceived liberalism of their seminary professors feel that their leaders (in some cases even their own parish pastors and priests) have left them. The perceived liberalism of these denominations has helped create a dramatic decline in their membership and attendance (save in the Catholic Church, which has been helped dramatically by the new wave of immigrants to America, largely with Catholic backgrounds). Those who have not disengaged themselves from the Christian faith in favor of the American way of "being good to yourself" have instead moved toward nondenominational churches, most of which are associated with the Right. Given the basic conservatism of these constituencies, and the feeling that they have been abandoned by their churches to the liberals, it is easy to see why politicians like Bush who can articulate their conservative agendas as "Christian crusades" against the liberals are likely to get the vote of these Christians, even those raised in families who worked or who still work nine-to-five union jobs. The perceived liberalism of these mainline churches' leadership has helped make Jesus and His Gospel conservative among American Protestants and Catholics who used to vote Democrat.

No two ways about it. In order to win these disgruntled mainline Christians back home and to more liberal ways of thinking, it will take a conservative theology, one that does not fall prey to the cultural trends that have turned them off. Such a faith perspective, claiming to provide a descriptive version of historic Christianity, would certainly function as a counter-cultural option to our twenty-first-century secularism. In fact, Christians holding such a viewpoint might even get more media attention were they able to articulate a viewpoint that remained faithful without seeming to embody the heritage of Fundamentalism, as the media often likes to remind us when trying to dismiss the Right's agenda.

How to do that with integrity? How to articulate a vision of the faith that is counter-cultural while still remaining in dialogue with the largely accepted scholarly conventions about history and the writing of the Bible? There are some options either forgotten or heretofore ignored by the mainline churches.

IT TAKES A CONSERVATIVE THEOLOGY TO FIND A LIBERAL JESUS: SOME FORGOTTEN OR IGNORED ALTERNATIVES

In his recent best seller, *God's Politics*, Jim Wallis pointed out how a literal reading of the Gospels and the rest of the Bible entails a strong concern for the plight of the poor. But as we previously pointed out, Wallis's proposals, largely given his nurture in churches associated with the Religious Right, continue to reflect suppositions of the Puritan Paradigm. Those of us not as readily confident as he seems to be about the historical veracity of all the Biblical accounts may also wonder if his perspective will really work for the clergy of these denominations or for their educated laity and for Secularists in the Democratic Party who might be willing to join such Christians in political coalitions. In fact there are at least two theological options that could help us articulate a conservative theology that has intellectual credibility and yet retains enough of the conservatism that the American public wants in its religion—is conservative enough to be counter-cultural in today's relativistic, therapeutic environment.

One of the available options has been around for nearly a century, with its origins in the first years after World War I. I refer to what is often called Neo-Orthodoxy, originated by the famous German-Swiss Reformed theologian Karl Barth (1886–1968). What he started gained many influential contemporaries of all denominational perspectives. This theology arrived in America before World War II, and by the 1950s was the dominant theological model in the seminaries and colleges of the mainline churches. Today, though, as our previous analysis of mainline theological education indicated, it is largely perceived in most of these circles as outdated and unable to address us in our context (save in some Midwestern Lutheran and Reformed bastions).

One suspects that Neo-Orthodoxy only lost its once-dominant perspective in the academy because of a combination of the growth of secularism's impact, the academy's increasingly intense infatuation with relativism, and the failure of this approach to have enough of an impact in parishes to keep the churches' leaders from abandoning it in favor of the theologically liberal endorsement of the new secular trends. It is odd, because an examination of the core Neo-Orthodox suppositions suggests that it offers a most intellectually credible counter-cultural alternative.

Barth and his allies were by no means out to repudiate the prevailing critical approaches to Scripture. But their commitment to reading the Bible literally was uncompromised. How to reconcile the miraculous realities portrayed by this ancient text with what we know about history, science, and medicine was his—as it is our—agenda. In order to do this, proponents of Neo-Orthodoxy draw on a nineteenth-century German concept, *Heilsgeschichte* (salvation-history). This idea allows the faithful to affirm the literal sense of the Bible's miracles even if these accounts are ruled on critically by historical and scientific criteria. The reason why these claims seem false, but are true, has to do with the character of God, it is argued. For God transcends all our human ways. Thus, when God enters the world, His Presence shatters all our categories. Consequently, the reason why the Biblical accounts concerning God do not make for good history or science is a function of the inadequacy of these conceptual tools for understanding God's Presence in the world. Tied to these suppositions was also an insistence that our understanding of the Bible is not a matter of your perspective, that it is possible for us to read and understand the Word of God together.[1]

Some of the factors in the failure of this viewpoint to have a cultural impact on the way American society views religion and Christianity in particular, despite the one-time dominance of this viewpoint in the academy during the mid-twentieth-century decades, have already been noted. Barth's Neo-Orthodoxy arrived in America just before the relativistic strands of thought associated with Kant, Weber, and other cutting-edge German Enlightenment thinkers came to be widely propagated in American university life after World War II. The more these philosophical and social scientific strands of thought filtered into mainline American theological education, the more Neo-Orthodoxy as a new kind of theological conservatism came under fire, eventually succumbing to the absolute relativism that is *the* politically correct worldview on most mainline seminary campuses.

The reason that makes the most sense to me, though, in trying to account for Neo-Orthodoxy's failure to have widespread social impact on America is that it has hardly ever been tried at the parish level. To this day, the concept of salvation-history is not one that is on the computer screen for most mainline American Christians, even those struggling with the truth of Biblical claims. Also unknown in the pews and in the larger culture is its concept that we can read the Word of God together when we are merely trying to exposit it, while taking into account the realities of relativism and different cultural or gender suppositions when the task is to meditate on the Word or preach it.

Neo-Orthodoxy's fidelity to objective truth, to the literal sense of the Bible's historylike accounts, and to the historic Creedal formulations of the Church certainly seems to lend itself to the need for a theologically conservative posture that will allow us to speak of the natural law's meaning, of the reality of Sin, with authority (for what is presented makes the audacious claim of being the Church's teaching, not just someone's perspective)—as well as in the counter-cultural way that will make the media and the public notice, and yet in an intellectually credible way that the opinion makers cannot easily explain away. Why don't we give it a try? This is a theological perspective, I hasten to add, that resisted Hitler and whose main proponent advocated the safety net of Socialism for the poor.[2]

The successor of Neo-Orthodoxy in America, emerging after its demise, might be termed Narrative (or Canonical) Theology. Led by several Yale University professors in the years after the 1960s, this style of theology affirms almost everything we found in Barth's legacy, save its concept of salvation-history. Instead of devising a concept of a special history, the advice of these Christian scholars is that we bracket questions of history and science when studying the Bible. It is not a Book of science and history, but a book about religion (2 Timothy 3:16).[3]

Although receiving much attention among scholars, the Narrative model of theology has not enjoyed the widespread impact among scholars that Neo-Orthodoxy received in its heyday. When it is considered in academic circles, the majority of scholars associated with the mainline denominations—and so ensconced in the relativism and skepticism of the modern academy and its culture—are critical. No less than Neo-Orthodoxy during the twentieth century, it is not yet receiving much attention at the parish level.

Perhaps this situation will change somewhat in view of the election of Pope Benedict XVI in 2005 (although at the time of publication of this book, the media and its celebration of relativism had yet to notice). For the present Pope has embraced many of the commitments of Narrative Theology, even citing with appreciation some proponents of this approach, contending that faith and technical knowledge must not be absorbed into each other.[4] With an ally like this one, who is perceived as conservative by the media, but without the charge of Fundamentalism, we may have a candidate for reviving mainline churches—someone with a theological perspective that can attract media attention and the attention of the pews, and who can be seen as an alternative to the theological liberalism of the seminaries. This theological model and its Neo-Orthodox ancestor will not let the relativism and Narcissism currently running wild among the elite in America have free reign in the Church and in society. It gives the faithful in the mainline denominations another alternative to this liberalism in their churches. It will be perceived as counter-cultural by the media elite—get their attention just as the new Pope has.

What is especially intriguing about this Narrative model is that it seems to connect with the pious in the American pews, according to recent poll data. This model's approach to the Bible as a text to be interpreted like a story, to be read literally, but with no corresponding affirmation of a Theory of Biblical Inerrancy, is in line with the piety of a most significant segment of the Democratic Party, the Black Church.[5] The Narrative approach's distinction between faith and scientific or historical knowledge addresses the disconnect in polls between the high numbers of those believing the Bible is inspired and should be read literally at least sometimes (77 percent of the public according to a May 2006 Gallup poll) and the results indicating that only one of two Americans believe that the Bible is totally accurate in all its teachings (as per a 2005 Barna Research poll and a 2005 Gallup poll on Evolution). The Narrative model allows us to address both the broader public's conservative theological bent while also not alienating those who would read the Bible critically regarding scientific and historical insights. This is a theological-religious perspective with a lot of potential to address a broad constituency.

With this Narrative Theological alternative, the Bush–Religious Right alternative will not be the only show in town. For the conservative, literalistic propensity of these theological perspectives will also give these churches a chance to educate their members and the society at large that Jesus and the religion that confesses Him are not conservative in the sense of the Republican economic agenda. Let's close now to talk about how it can happen.

Conclusion: Where Do We Go from Here?

To my mind Jim Wallis and Michael Lerner have gone a long way toward answering the question I have posed in this title. Their call to religious people to organize a movement of the Left to counter the Right's policies makes good sense.[1] Their proposals to form an interfaith movement is certainly in the tradition of the successful strategies of Martin Luther King Jr. and the Civil Rights Movement. The Religious Right has done it with impressive success. It's time for socially concerned faithful of the Left to get in gear.

This book, though, has pointed out some other homework we need to do. Besides getting organized in Political Action Committees and lobbying local Democratic Party headquarters to act like Democrats (good short-term strategies), we can also help the cause long-term by organizing religious education opportunities in our own religious communities, helping them to see that the politically conservative version of the faith (of Jesus in the case of Christians) is not to be found in the literal sense of the Biblical text. Of course this approach will meet some resistance, as for every text we cite about the need to work for peace and for the sake of the poor, there will be those who take up the issues of individual morality (pro-life, anti-gay teachings) in the name of your tradition. This is where this book can be of some immediate help, both with regard to how to read your sacred texts literally in an intellectually credible way, but also to help remove some of the barriers to seeing that your religious traditions are in no way a barrier to progressive politics. Let's review these points in closing.

We've noticed that the main roadblock to getting Jesus, His Gospel, and other religious traditions out of the "conservative box" has to do

147

with the fact that the Religious Right has capitalized on the suppositions of America's Puritan Paradigm. That is to say, most Americans at least subconsciously read the Bible in light of the suppositions of the "individualized" Puritanism, tempered by Revivalism, which has effectively functioned as America's "civil religion" at least since the nineteenth century (the religious values and rhetoric that are closely associated with American self-identity). What seems to be common sense for most Americans about the Bible and religion is really this Revivalist-tempered Puritanism. By getting the public to hear their version of Jesus as the fulfillment of this American version of Puritanism, the Right has most people convinced that its version of religion and the politics associated with it must be true.

If you can't lick 'em, join 'em. Even after helping your fellow members to see the Puritan suppositions of much of their thinking, the reality is that these suppositions are so embedded in the worldview of most Americans that they are not going to go away. This book has pointed out how a political coalition of the Left might develop rhetoric and policies that trade in on some of these deeply embedded suppositions and still keep its progressive soul. Start teaching people about the natural law and the doctrine of Original Sin. But do it in a conservative way, take the ideas literally, and mind what your tradition has historically said about them. These are Christian concepts that can also communicate outside the Christian community to the public as a whole. We've seen that they are core concepts of the Constitution. Get that word out to your religious community and the community as a whole. The Right won't do it; spreading that knowledge is not in their interests.

WHAT TO TEACH AND
WHAT DIFFERENCE IT CAN MAKE

If we could educate American Christians—the American public as a whole—to the concepts of natural law and Sin, it would be good for the Left, for the cause of justice, and for American society as a whole. At the very least, as we have noted, understanding these concepts would better educate all Americans in the core suppositions of our Constitutional system.

We have already noted how, contrary to Bill Press and some other critics, the content of the natural law is virtually identical with the Second Table of the Ten Commandments (those Commandments dealing with our responsibility toward our fellow human beings).[2] It strikes me that there are rich possibilities here for dealing with the whole controversy over displaying the Commandments on public property. Wouldn't permitting displays of the Second Table take the heat out of the controversy? Literally, they do not refer to God. In any case, a renewed stress on the natural law provides Jews, Christians, and Muslims with an excellent opportunity for religious education for their flocks. And when that happens, at least from an ecumenical Christian point of view (Jews and Muslims are already largely in the Democratic camp), these Commandments have historically been interpreted in ways most friendly to the idea of government safety nets for the poor, pro-labor, and managed economic policies.

Here and in the previous discussion I have deliberately not spent much time referring to how the Commandment "Thou shall not kill" relates to abortion and how the Commandment against adultery relates to homosexuality. That is the Right's hang-up. Its proponents want us to get hung up on these issues (leaving the economy and foreign policy alone). If our task is to instruct our religious communities and American society as a whole about the natural law and its meaning, we will realize that these two Commandments are only part of an overall picture that concerns theft (making sure that the market is not victimizing anyone), lying (interpreted as a call for justice, truth, and access in the community's [and its media's] communication), and coveting (ensuring that we are not a society unduly materialistic in its aims and goals, one that encourages us to cut corners to gain what we want). If family values are what you want, do not forget that each of these traditions interpret the Commandment concerning the honoring of mother and father to be reciprocal, to involve adults' responsibility to children, both spiritually and physically. If these Commandments were obeyed, every American child would have a quality education, quality health care, and be out of poverty. These Commandments certainly do not hurt the causes of the Left.

As for the Commandments about murder and adultery, we previously noted how little attention Jesus and the Bible give to abortion and committed homosexual relations. But even if the Right is correct about these activities as in contrast to the natural law, a full teaching of these Commandments would also entail new commitments on the part of their adherents to cracking down on the sex trade, pornography, higher wages for the working poor, and welfare checks that would guarantee higher standards of living.³ If our concern is to maintain family values—to protect marriage—then we need to come to terms with all the sociological research that indicates that poverty is one of the greatest enemies of successful marriages.⁴ And so I challenge my colleagues in the religious leadership and the political pros: What are we waiting for? These traditional interpretations of the Commandments are news—if we learn how to "spin" them.

A word of advice: Perhaps we do not need to talk about teaching the natural law to many of our constituencies. How about lessons on our "common morality" or "common sense," helping the public to understand that all the "rights" we hold dear (the "life, liberty and pursuit of happiness" trinity, along with free speech, civil rights, and the like) are all rooted in the Commandments we all know concerning strictures on murder, theft, lying, mistrust, and respect for authority? Those headlines are likely to work better, to get some media attention (particularly if we posed the project as a response to the Right's religiosity/theocracy). Meanwhile, back in the church or synagogue, calling these lessons on the Decalogue or Torah is just fine.

Of course, we might not want to emphasize too much that the public needs a reeducation on the Christian doctrine of Sin. That could lose the Democratic Secular and Jewish base. How about Constitutional education on the Founders' fear about the perils of selfishness and self-interest? In view of George Bush's justification for international policies as what is in accord with American interests, it's time to educate us all on what it's all about. Self-interest is Sin! Likewise on the domestic scene, what's good for business is not necessarily in the interests of the labor force, or for the nation as a whole for that matter. The Founders of our nation taught that! You read the texts in chapter 9; let's get this word out. The Founders of our nation were open to redistributing wealth.

Religious congregations, caught up in a therapeutic legalism that has taught most religious Americans that they can save themselves (as per a 2005 Barna Research poll indicating that over one in two Americans think that we earn a place in heaven by what we do), also badly need these lessons. They need these lessons if we are to recover and nurture a need for God's forgiving love and grace.

An awareness of the doctrine of Sin and the way in which its view of human nature entails the need for checks and balances on the interests of those in power is a valuable a lesson for the Democratic Party leadership. These insights challenge the policies of the Clinton-Gore-Lieberman Democratic Leadership Council (the so-called New Democrats), who have taken the Party away from advocating for the interests of organized labor, discouraging the language of "class warfare" in favor of currying support from liberal white-collar professionals. Thomas Frank is right: Given this drift, as long as it continues, the issues motivating the Democratic Party of Roosevelt and his heirs will be off the table for American policy makers—unless we can recover an awareness that class interests will clash and that only in the struggle between these factions can we approach something like (imperfect) justice.[5]

We need to get the media to notice the Christian doctrine of Sin, stressing its roots in the Constitution—lest these insights fracture any emerging coalition with non-Christian segments of the electorate—and its implications for a healthy suspicion about ourselves, our aims, and our institutions. Though these insights will help the Left (this is the kind of religion that is good for Democrats), it is also good news for the Right. These insights also teach healthy suspicion of government monopolies, just as the natural law also reminds Americans of their own responsibilities before God and each other. Renewed stress on these doctrines is good for the Church, to help it get Jesus away from the Right, and good for the Democratic Party—but also good for America as a whole. So let's start teaching these concepts, advocating and marketing them in collaboration with other activists. But we need to keep these Constitutionally rooted religious ideas at the forefront, or the media and even some of our allies on the Left will start hearing us as trying to impose religion on the state no less than the Right. So take the natural law and Sin with you in your activism (and be sure to bring your fellow religious adherents with you).

THE SILENCED (RELIGIOUS) MAJORITY: ISN'T IT TIME THE DEMOCRATS AND THE MEDIA STOPPED IGNORING THEM?

Another message of this book to the political pros regarding where we go from here is that we dare not continue to ignore the mainline Protestant denominations, even if the media is wont to do so. Why the media fails to notice this large segment of the American population is a story for another book. I have already given some hints. The new theology that has come to dominate these denominations and the impact it has had on church life, coupled with the media's own saturation with the values of Enlightenment Relativism are all contributing factors in the "silent treatment." The media, after all, is still drinking deeply in a "secularized" version of the Puritan Paradigm (with the old Protestant work ethic stressing results and visible success, now tempered with the therapeutic absolution of guilt, a modernist reaction against the old Puritan morality, and naturalistic account of Providence). Evangelicals and Fundamentalists are news because they challenge the media's new version of American life, and the media loves conflict (as long as it can paint the adversary into a corner, which it gladly does in the case of the Religious Right). The Black Church and Catholic Church are also news, because they largely challenge the Puritan Paradigm or don't quite fit in (in the case of the former). Likewise the Amish and other sects. But mainline Protestantism has pretty much accepted the evolution of the Puritan Paradigm as the media and cultural elites have adjusted it, but always behind these opinion makers—as followers, not leaders.

For all these reasons, the mainline Protestant denominations are not news. These dynamics also contribute to the politicians' general neglect of these constituencies. Besides, for reasons we have noted, the leaders of these denominations cannot deliver votes like the Southern Baptists and other Evangelical bodies can.

It is hardly surprising that since Bush and the Republicans began winning the religious vote, political commentators began paying attention to American religion. But in view of all the factors we have noted, it is little wonder that when these commentators take up the subject of religion, they have neglected the mainline and the Puritan roots of American religion. I have already taken Kevin Phillips to task for his concentration on the so-called sectarian character of American religion and on the Evangelical Movement, with the related contention that the old mainline establishment is virtually irrelevant. He is not alone in this error among political pundits, as is evident in every hitherto published book calling American Christians and the Democratic Party to form new coalitions. Mainline Protestants and Catholic realities are ignored.

Let's look at the data again. If we consider Evangelical-related denominations, we have at best 40 million members. But when we consider the coalition among the Black Church, mainline Protestantism, Eastern Orthodoxy, and the Catholic Church (a coalition that has a history of voting Democrat at least from Roosevelt until the Reagan Revolution, and since the beginnings of the modern ecumenical movement are the more natural coalition partners than any of these bodies would be with the Religious Right), the total membership is over 102 million. Get that? Although I concede that in the long run the future may be dim for many of these denominations unless they get on board with the developments I propose, and the most Puritanized of these denominations (especially Episcopalians) have a history of voting Republican, the mainline Protestant–Black Church–Roman Catholic coalition outnumbers the Religious Right by nearly three to one (and the mainline denominations alone are only outnumbered by the Right by four to three, presupposing, which you can't, that every Southern Baptist or mega-church member votes Republican). Those are the statistics that count for those who want to win in the next elections. History shows that, with the right kind of theological marketing (notably in the 1930s among Northern Baptists and Northern Presbyterians, and again in the 1960s in most mainline churches based in the North in support of Civil Rights Movement), even voters in the most Puritan-related of these denominations (at least those in metropolitan congregations) have displayed an openness to big-government efforts to aid the distressed.[6]

No two ways about it: If you want to keep America's Jesus conservative and Republican, don't heed these warnings, keep ignoring the mainline religious bodies, and worry about personal morality and your own enhanced prosperity. But then don't expect anyone but the rich and powerful to profit.

Notes

ACKNOWLEDGMENTS

1. Given my irenic perspective, I cannot endorse the recent harsh critique of the Religious Right by Chris Hedges, *American Fascists: The Christian Right and War in America* (New York: Free Press, 2006), even though I might agree with his politics.

INTRODUCTION

1. Charles Krauthammer, "Mild Swing, Not Realignment," *Atlanta Journal-Constitution*, November 10, 2006, A13. For exit poll data, see Pew Research Center Observation Deck, "Centrists Deliver for Democrats," November 8, 2006, at pewreseach.org/obdeck=88. Even in categories of religious voters among whom Democrats significantly enhanced their approval in the 2007 elections, such as nearly cutting in half the previous Republican advantage over Democrats among weekly church-goers, Republicans still held a healthy 12 percent point advantage with this group.

2. Walter Rauschenbusch, *Christianity and Social Crisis* (New York: Macmillan, 1907); Martin Luther King Jr., "Facing the Challenge of a New Age," *Phylon* (April 1957): 24–34.

3. For examples of Wallis's efforts to reinterpret Christianity as a prophetic religion and his tendency to privilege Christian convictions in society, see his *God's Politics: Why the Right Gets It Wrong and the Left Doesn't Get It* (New York: HarperSanFrancisco, 2005), pp. 72–84, 209ff. Also see Bob Edgar, *Middle Church: Reclaiming the Moral Values of the Faithful Majority from the Religious Right* (New York: Simon & Schuster, 2006), especially pp. 195ff; Randall Balmer, *Thy Kingdom Come: How the Religious Right Distorts the Faith and Threatens America* (New York: Basic, 2006), especially pp. 175–77,

190–91; Michael Lerner, *The Left Hand of God: Taking Back Our Country from the Religious Right* (New York: HarperSanFrancisco, 2006), especially pp. 213ff; Kathleen Kennedy Townsend, *Failing America's Faithful: How Today's Churches Are Mixing God with Politics and Losing Their Way* (New York: Warner Books, 2007), pp. 27–29, 125–27. John Danforth, *Faith and Politics: How the "Moral Values" Debate Divides America and How to Move Forward* (New York: Viking, 2006), especially p. 10, also finds Wallis identifying his political proposals with Christian teaching.

4. Bill Press, *How the Republicans Stole Christmas: The Republican Party's Declared Monopoly on Religion and What Democrats Can Do to Take It Back* (New York: Doubleday, 2005), especially pp. 240–41, appeals as I do to the natural law as a Constitutionally authorized way to have one's religion impact politics. But he does not elaborate all the implications of this point, and he overlooks another Constitutionally rooted point of overlap between Christian faith and politics—the sinful, concupiscent character of human beings.

Also see Barack Obama, *The Audacity of Hope: Thoughts on Reclaiming the American Dream* (New York: Crown, 2006), especially pp. 86, 214–15. Jimmy Carter, *Our Endangered Values: America's Moral Crisis* (New York: Simon & Schuster, 2005), especially pp. 18, 57–64, likewise seems to appeal to something like the natural law by referring to a common morality that nations and religious organizations can share. But these authors do not identify this concept, and Carter even mixes it with a Puritan-like appeal to distinct Christian (New Testament) teachings (see p. 152). Similar strengths and weaknesses can be attributed to Gregory A. Boyd, *The Myth of a Christian Nation: How the Quest for Political Power Is Destroying the Church* (Grand Rapids, MI: Zondervan, 2005), especially pp. 14–15, 35–44, 127–41. With the possible exception of Boyd, all of these authors likewise overlook, as Press fails to recognize, the contribution that the doctrine of Sin can make to progressive politics.

John Danforth, *Faith and Politics* (2006), especially pp. 15–16, 218–20, is in the same spirit as the above authors in insisting that faith does not tell us with specificity what political positions to take. But like the previous authors he neither invokes the natural law nor the doctrine of Sin. Also see Jon Meacham, *American Gospel* (New York: Random House, 2006), especially pp. 13, 25.

Another book that I would similarly praise for its emphasis on natural law and Constitutional perspective for authorizing progressive Christian engagement in politics is Mel White, *Religion Gone Bad: The Hidden Dangers of the Christian Right* (New York: Torcher/Penguin, 2006), especially pp. 249ff. But like the other authors he does not explore the contribution the doctrine of Sin can make to a progressive politics and he does not offer any strategies for building voting coalitions with Christians outside the Evangelical Movement.

Ray Suarez, *The Holy Vote: The Politics of Faith in America* (New York: HarperCollins, 2006), especially pp. 22–23, 262, 298–99, moves in similar directions in trying to maintain church-state separation. But he incorrectly does this by effectively rejecting the concept of natural law (see pp. 112–14), because he has unwittingly come to understand religion in Puritan categories as necessarily entailing that its adherents will seek to legislate distinct Christian values. He is correct, though, in contending that our national life is shaped by both secular and Christian suppositions. I have provided verification for that contention in my *A Common Sense Theology: The Bible, Faith, and American Society* (Macon, GA: Mercer University Press, 1995), pp. 104–33.

5. Kevin Phillips, *American Theocracy: The Peril and Politics of Radical Religion, Oil, and Borrowed Money in the 21st Century* (New York: Viking, 2006), pp. 100ff (and especially p. 104); Chris Hedges, *American Fascists: The Christian Right and War in America* (New York: Free Press, 2006), especially pp. 11–12, 18–20. Even if we use Phillips's and Hedges's survey statistics regarding the percentage of voters who are affiliated with Conservative Evangelical churches (Phillips, pp. 106, 114, 119; Hedges, pp. 18–20), exit polling indicates that a greater portion of the electorate belongs to a coalition of mainline Protestant, black Protestant, and Catholic Christians. Phillips also overlooks that, historically, the sects he cites in supporting his claim have over decades adopted the more staid ways and lifestyle of American Puritanism.

For similar neglect of the impact of building coalitions that reach out to mainline churchgoers, see Douglas B. Sosnik, Matthew J. Dowd, and Ron Fournier, *Applebee's America: How Successful Political, Business, and Religious Leaders Connect with the New American Community* (New York: Simon & Schuster, 2006), especially p. 100. Ray Suarez, in *Holy Vote*, also neglects the political clout of the mainline denominations.

6. Even the primary advocate of understanding American history in relation to the Puritan Paradigm, Sydney E. Ahlstrom, *A Religious History of the American People* (New Haven, CT: Yale University Press, 1972), p. 1079, concedes that in some sense the 1960s brought us into a post-Puritan ethos. Of course on p. 1086, he also contends in response to late 1960s survey data that most adult Americans still held older Puritan convictions in an outward sense.

CHAPTER 1

1. Sydney E. Ahlstrom, *A Religious History of the American People* (New Haven, CT: Yale University Press, 1972), pp. 3, 12, 1079, 1094–96; H. Richard Niebuhr, *The Kingdom of God in America* (New York: Harper & Row, 1937), especially pp. 8, 45ff.; Mark Noll, "The Luther Difference," *First Things*, February 1992, p. 38; cf. Mark Ellingsen, *Blessed Are the Cynical: How Original Sin Can Make America a Better Place* (Grand Rapids, MI: Brazos, 2003), pp. 43–44.

2. See Max Weber, *Die Protestantische Ethik und der Geist der Kapitalismus* (Archiv fur Sozialwissenschaft und Sozialpolitik, 1904–1905); Ernst Troeltsch, *The Social Teachings of the Christian Churches*, trans. Olive Wyon (New York: Allen & Unwin, 1931). For Calvin's reflections on the role of disciplined living as a sign of election, see his *Institutio Christianae Religionis* (1559), III.XX.1–2; III.XXIV.17.

3. This understanding of American Christianity in terms of the planting of the Kingdom of God in America was most compellingly articulated by Niebuhr, *Kingdom of God*, xii–xiii. This preoccupation with advancing the Kingdom was expressly rooted in Puritanism in *The Westminster Confession of Faith* (1647), X.4. Early American Puritans expressly voiced this conviction regarding extending the Kingdom of God to American shores; see William Bradford, in William T. Davis, ed., *Bradford's History of the Plymouth Plantation* (New York: Scribner, 1920), p. 46. But see Gen. 6:6; Mark 6:5; [Lutheran] *Formula of Concord* (1577), SDVIII.20–21.

4. See www.barna.org. A May 8–11, 2006, Gallup poll identifies over 70 percent of the public as regarding the Bible as in some sense the inspired Word of God. See pollingreport.com/religion.htm.

5. A similar construal of the role of the state in relation to furthering Christian commitments was articulated a decade later in *The Fundamental Orders of Connecticut* (1639). See the polls results in the Pew Forum on Religion and Public Life, "Religion and Politics: Contention and Consensus (Part II)," 2003, at pewforum/index. When Kathleen Kennedy Townsend [*Failing America's Faithful: How Today's Churches Are Mixing God with Politics and Losing Their Way* (New York: Warner Books, 2007), pp. 94–95] praises the social consciousness of Puritanism, she overlooks this commitment as well as the pro-capitalist sympathies of the leaders of the movement that we will examine.

6. *Reliquiae Baxterianae; or, Mr. Richard Baxter's Narrative of the Most Memorable Passages of His Life and Times* (1696), p. 30. For this point I am indebted to Robert Paul, *The Assembly of the Lord* (Edinburgh: T & T Clark, 1985), pp. 5–6, 25.

7. R. H. Tawney, *Religion and the Rise of Capitalism: A Historical Study* (New York: Harcourt Brace, 1926), pp. 235–36.

8. Richard Steele, *The Tradesman's Calling, Being a Discourse Concerning the Nature, Necessity, Choice, etc., of a Calling in General* (1684), p. 22.

9. Henry Ward Beecher, quoted in Ahlstrom, *A Religious History*, p. 789.

10. Joseph Lee, *A Vindication of a Regulated Enclosure* (1656), p. 9; Cotton Mather, *Magnalia Christi Americana*, vol. 1 (1702; repr., Hartford, 1853), p. 61.

11. Michael Lerner, *The Left Hand of God* (New York: HarperSanFrancisco, 2006), pp. 1–3, 109–10.

12. For example, see *Second London Confession* (1677/1688), pp. I, III, V.1, X.1, XIX.4–6, XXIV.2; *The New Hampshire Confession* (1833), pp. i, ix, xi, xvi.

13. Baron de Montesquieu, *Spirit of the Laws* (1748). On his impact on the Founders, see David A. J. Richards, *Foundations of American Constitutionalism* (New York: Oxford University Press, 1989), pp. 122, 123, 127–29; also see my *Blessed Are the Cynical*, pp. 54–55.

The Westminster Confession, VI; cf. James Madison, "No. 10" and "No. 51," in *The Federalist Papers* (New York: Mentor, 1961), pp. 77–84, 324–25; Alexander Hamilton, "No. 71," *Federalist Papers*, p. 432.

14. John Witherspoon, *An Annotated Edition of Lectures on Moral Philosophy*, ed. Jack Scott (Newark: University of Delaware Press, 1982), p. 144.

15. On the Deism of a number of the Founders, see David L. Holmes, *The Faiths of the Founding Fathers* (Oxford, UK: Oxford University Press, 2006), especially pp. 49ff. For Benjamin Franklin's qualified Deism, see his "On the Providence of God in the Government of the World" (1730), in *Writings* (New York: Library of America, 1987), pp. 165–68. See also Thomas Jefferson, "Letter to Dr. Benjamin Waterhouse" (1822), in *Writings* (New York: Library of America, 1984), pp. 1458–59; James Madison, "Letter to Frederick Beasley" (1825), in *Writings*, vol. 9 (New York: Putnam, 1910), pp. 229–31.

On the impact of Scottish Common Sense Realism on the Founders and on the Puritan Paradigm, see Mark Noll, *America's God: From Jonathan Edwards to Abraham Lincoln* (New York: Oxford University Press, 2002), pp. 93–113; Sydney E. Ahlstrom, "The Scottish Philosophy and American Theology," *Church History* 24 (1955): 257–72; Gary Wills, *Inventing America: Jefferson's Declaration of Independence* (New York: Vintage, 1979), especially pp. 181–92, 237–38, 288–89. The Founders seem to rely on something like this philosophy in the Declaration of Independence's references to "self-evident truths." See Thomas Jefferson, *Letter to Peter Carr* (1787) in *Writings* (New York: The Library of America), pp. 181 ff.

CHAPTER 2

1. For this characterization of the relation between Revivalism and the African-American Church, see Albert J. Raboteau, *Canaan Land: A Religious History of African Americans* (Oxford, UK: Oxford University Press, 1999, 2001), p. 103. For the classical statement of American Revivalism's social impact, see Timothy Smith, *Revivalism and Social Reform in Nineteenth Century America* (Nashville, TN: Abingdon, 1957).

2. For this assessment, see Bruce J. Evensen, *God's Man for the Gilded Age: D. L. Moody and the Rise of Modern Mass Evangelism* (Oxford, UK: Oxford University Press, 2003), p. 187. Evensen also notes the impact of Moody's methods on Sunday.

3. Jonathan Edwards, *Christian Charity; or, The Duty of Charity to the Poor, Explained and Enforced* (n.d.), II ff., in *Works*, vol. 2 (Peabody, MA:

Hendrickson, 1998), pp. 164–73; Jonathan Edwards, *Some Thoughts Concerning the Present Revival* (n.d.), II.I; V.II; V.III, in *Works*, vol. 1, pp. 381–82, 425–26, 430. Edwards may have backed away later in his career from this identification of Americans with the chosen people, at least to the point of expressing disappointment with the subsequent outcomes of the Awakening in New England, but the influence of his earlier position was never compromised. For an interpretation contending that Edwards totally renounced belief in America's choseness, see Mark Noll, *America's God: From Jonathan Edwards to Abraham Lincoln* (New York: Oxford University Press, 2002), pp. 47–48. But in the very text cited to support this conclusion, Edwards only went so far as to express disappointment in the revival's outcome and to qualify the sense in which the Awakening was a forerunner of the End. See Jonathan Edwards, *Letter to Rev. Mr. McCulloch* (1744) in *Works*, vol. 1, pp. cxx–cxxi.

   4. Charles G. Finney, *Memoirs...* (New York: A. S. Barnes, 1879), p. 442. Also see Charles G. Finney, "Letters on Revivals—No. 23" (n.d.), quoted in Donald W. Dayton, *Discovering an Evangelical Heritage* (New York: Harper & Row, 1976), pp. 20–24. For more on Finney's condemnation of slavery, see his *Lectures on Revivals* (New York, 1835), pp. 265–66, 271; though there is evidence of his prejudice. See Charles Finney, "Letter to Arthur Tappan," April 30, 1836, Finney Papers, Oberlin College Library. For a different assessment of Finney, regarding his lack of a public social justice emphasis, see Douglas W. Frank, *Less than Conquerors: How Evangelicals Entered the Twentieth Century* (Grand Rapids, MI: Eerdmans, 1986), p. 24.

   Early leaders in the crusade for Women's Suffrage who were activated in this way include Sarah Grimke, Angelina Grimke, Elizabeth Cady Stanton, and Susan B. Anthony. See Dayton, *Discovering an Evangelical Heritage*, pp. 89ff.

   5. Among the strongest proponents of this way of interpreting the heritage of the Holiness Movement include Dayton, *Discovering an Evangelical Heritage*, pp. 76ff.

   6. See John Farwell, *The Secret of Success* (1889), in William G. McLoughlin Jr., *Modern Revivalism: Charles Grandison Finney to Billy Graham* (New York: Ronald Press, 1959), pp. 267–68.

   7. For these insights about Moody's fund-raising style I am indebted to Lewis A. Drummond, "D. L. Moody and Revivalism," in *Mr. Moody and the Evangelical Tradition*, ed. Timothy George (London: T & T Clark, 2004), p. 92.

   8. Dwight Moody, quoted in *Boston Daily Advertiser*, February 12, 1877, p. 4.

   9. Dwight Moody, "The Workingman and His Foes," *Christian Advocate*, March 4, 1875, p. 68.

   10. Dwight Moody, *The Great Redemption* (Chicago: Merchants' Speciality Co.), pp. 355–56.

11. McLoughlin, *Modern Revivalism*, pp. 274, 277. On Chapman's practices, see p. 385.

12. Dwight Moody, "The Gateway into the Kingdom," in *The Way to God and How to Find It* (Chicago: Moody Press, 1884), p. 33. For this characterization of Moody's thought in general I am indebted to Sydney E. Ahlstrom, *A Religious History of the American People* (New Haven, CT: Yale University Press, 1972), p. 745. See n. 17, below.

13. Dwight Moody, quoted in McLoughlin, *Modern Revivalism*, p. 277.

14. Moody, *The Way to God*, p. 23.

15. Dwight Moody, quoted in George M. Marsden, *Fundamentalism and American Culture: The Shaping of Twentieth-Century Evangelicalism 1870–1925* (Oxford, UK: Oxford University Press, 1980), pp. 36–37.

16. McLoughlin, *Modern Revivalism*, pp. 248, 249.

17. Dwight Moody, *Lectures on Revivals of Religion* (n.p.: E. J. Goodrich, 1868), p. 9; Dwight Moody, "The Reward of the Faithful," in *Great Joy* (New York: E. B. Treat, 1877), pp. 21ff.; Dwight Moody, "Perseverance," in *"To All People"* (New York: E. B. Treat, 1877), p. 166. Also see Thomas Jefferson, "Letter to William Green Mumford" (1799) in *Writings,* pp. 1064–66.

18. Dwight Moody, "The Second Coming of Christ," in *"To All People,"* pp. 508–9. Also see Donald Dayton, "The Social and Political Conservatism of Modern American Evangelicalism: A Preliminary Search for the Reasons," *Union Seminary Quarterly Review* 32, no. 2 (Winter 1977): 78. Cf. Charles G. Finney, "Letters on Revivals—No. 23," *The Oberlin Evangelist* 8 (January 21, 1846): 11.

19. Lawrence County Historical Society, *The Ira D. Sankey Centenary: Proceedings of the Centenary Celebration of the Birth of Ira D. Sankey Together with Some Hitherto Unpublished Sankey Correspondence* (New Castle, PA: Lawrence County Historical Society, 1941), p. 55; Ira D. Sankey, *My Life and the Story of the Gospel Hymns* (Philadelphia, 1907), p. 88.

20. Kevin Phillips, *American Theocracy: The Peril and Politics of Radical Religion, Oil, and Borrowed Money in the 21st Century* (New York: Viking, 2006), especially pp. 1–5.

21. Dwight Moody, quoted in McLoughlin, *Modern Revivalism*, p. 275.

22. Dwight Moody, quoted in McLoughlin, *Modern Revivalism*, p. 246.

23. See McLoughlin, *Modern Revivalism*, 348ff., on the revolt against Revivals, leading to the Social Gospel Movement. For the assessment of Moody's impact on subsequent Revivalism, see Evensen, *God's Man*, p. 187.

24. Billy Sunday, "Sermon to Businessmen," in Sunday Papers, Winona Lake, IN.

25. Billy Sunday, quoted in Edwin S. Gaustad, ed., *A Documentary History of Religion in America Since 1865* (Grand Rapids, MI: Eerdmans, 1993), p. 291; Billy Sunday, quoted in *Boston Herald*, November 14, 1916, p. 5.

26. See McLoughlin, *Modern Revivalism*, p. 432. For the quotation, see Billy Sunday, quoted in McLoughlin, *Modern Revivalism*, p. 435.

27. Billy Sunday, quoted in McLoughlin, *Modern Revivalism*, p. 428.

28. For examples of Sunday's pro-business, antilabor orientation, see McLoughlin, *Modern Revivalism*, pp. 440, 442; *New York Times*, May 20, 1916, p. 10. For revivals as the cure for poverty, see Sunday's quotations in *Boston Herald*, January 12, 1917, p. 3; *Boston Herald*, December 14, 1916, p. 5.

29. Billy Sunday, quoted in Ahlstrom, *A Religious History*, p. 748; Billy Sunday, quoted in Providence *News*, October 2, 1918, p. 12.

30. See McLoughlin, *Modern Revivalism*, p. 433, for this characterization of Sunday's thought. Also see pp. 364–65 for a list of these Revivalists who shared Sunday's mixing of nationalism and faith.

31. Billy Sunday, quoted in *Boston Herald*, November 20, 1916, p. 5.

32. Billy Sunday, in *Boston Herald*, December 4, 1916, p. 4.

33. Billy Sunday, in *Pittsburgh Press*, January 4, 1914, Edit. Sec., 8. For his support of Prohibition, see McLoughlin, *Modern Revivalism*, pp. 412–13, 439–40; Ahlstrom, *A Religious History*, p. 903.

34. See McLoughlin, *Modern Revivalism*, pp. 452–54. For data on the educational level of the constituencies of Republican-voting, churchgoing Christians, see the Pew Research Center for the People and the Press, Survey Reports, "Profile of Religious Groups," May 1996. In "The Diminishing Divide: American Churches, American Politics," at http://people-press.org/reports. June 25, 1996. There is little reason to think that demographics have changed radically in the last decade.

35. Billy Graham, "Sermon of the Month: Spiritual Inventory" (Minneapolis, MN: Billy Graham Evangelistic Association, 1955); Billy Graham, *Decision, Newsletter of the Billy Graham Evangelistic Association* (Minneapolis, March 1956); Billy Graham, "Sermon of the Month: The Revival We Need" (Minneapolis, MN: Billy Graham Evangelistic Association, 1956).

36. Billy Graham, "The Unfinished Dream," *Christianity Today*, July 31, 1970, p. 20.

37. Reinhold Niebuhr, "A Proposal to Billy Graham," *Christian Century*, August 8, 1956, p. 921. For the characterization of Graham's reluctance to condemn social sins, see Mark A. Noll, *American Evangelical Christianity: An Introduction* (Malden, MA: Blackwell, 2001), p. 50.

38. Billy Graham, "Why Lausanne?" *Christianity Today*, September 13, 1974, p. 12; cf. Billy Graham, *Angels: God's Secret Angels* (New York: Doubleday, 1975). For his strategy on how to effect social change, see Billy Graham, "What Ten Years Have Taught Me," *Christian Century*, February 17, 1960, pp. 187, 188.

39. Billy Graham, quoted in *New York Herald Tribune*, May 12, 1957, p. 24. For his views on poverty, see Robert B. Fowler, *A New Engagement:*

Evangelical Political Thought, 1966–1976 (Grand Rapids, MI: Eerdmans, 1982), p. 48.

40. Fowler, *A New Engagement*, p. 46, provides the more characteristically Graham-friendly portrayal of the matter; McLoughlin, *Modern Revivalism*, p. 505, with supporting documentation, offers the more critical version of the data.

41. Billy Graham, "Partners with God" (n.d.), in McLoughlin, *Modern Revivalism*, 520.

42. See Fowler, *New Engagement*, pp. 48, 256.

43. Billy Graham, quoted in McLoughlin, *Modern Revivalism*, p. 509.

44. Billy Graham, "Address to the NAE Convention" (1952), quoted in McLoughlin, *Modern Revivalism*, pp. 483–84.

45. These dynamics, not Dispensationalism or undue realism, as Michael Lerner alleges in his *The Left Hand of God: Taking Back Our Country from the Religious Right* (New York: HarperSanFrancisco, 2005), pp. 95–96, 110ff., accounts for the Religious Right's coalition with neoconservative policies.

46. See chap. 1, n. 15, for references.

47. For these insights I am indebted to Mark Noll, "The Lutheran Difference," *First Things*, February 1992; William A. Clebsch, *From Sacred to Profane America: The Role of Religion in American History* (repr.; Chico, CA: Scholars Press, 1968), especially p. ix.

48. For this insight I am indebted to H. Richard Niebuhr, *The Kingdom of God in America* (New York: Harper & Row, 1937), pp. 86–87. For an example of the presence of these commitments in the Constitution, see James Madison, "No. 51," *The Federalist Papers* (New York: Mentor, 1961), pp. 324–25.

CHAPTER 3

1. For this analysis I am indebted to William G. McLoughlin, *Modern Revivalism: Charles Grandison Finney to Billy Graham* (New York: Ronald Press, 1959), pp. 464ff.

2. For a more detailed analysis of these dynamics and those subsequently described, see my book, *The Evangelical Movement: Growth, Impact, Controversy, Dialog* (Minneapolis, MN: Augsburg, 1988), pp. 66ff.

3. For a good example of the views of this segment of early Fundamentalism, see the Niagara Creed (1878), a document drawn up by a number of the leaders of the Niagara Conference, one of the Bible and Prophetic Conferences that effectively organized the Fundamentalist Movement.

4. A. A. Hodge and B. B. Warfield, "Inspiration," in *Princeton Theology 1812–1921*, ed. Mark A. Noll (Grand Rapids, MI: Baker Books, 1983), pp. 221ff.

5. Charles Hodge, "The War," *Princeton Review* (1863): 14. For this analysis I am indebted to Donald Dayton, "The Social and Political Conservatism of

Modern American Evangelicalism: A Preliminary Search for the Reasons," *Union Seminary Quarterly Review* 32, no. 2 (Winter 1977): 76–77.

6. "Foreword," *The Fundamentals: Testimony to the Truth*, vol. 1 (Chicago: Testimony Publishing, n.d.), p. 4.

7. The credit for coining the term belongs to Curtis Lee Laws, "Convention Side Lights," *Watchman Examiner* 8 (July 1, 1920), p. 834.

8. Sources for this faulty stereotype include Stewart G. Cole, *The History of Fundamentalism* (New York: Richard R. Smith, 1931); Norman F. Furniss, *The Fundamentalist Controversy, 1918–1931* (New Haven, CT: Yale University Press, 1954); H. Richard Niebuhr, "Fundamentalism," *Encyclopedia of Social Sciences*, vol. 6 (New York, 1937), pp. 526–27.

9. References to the favorable hearing given by the secular and liberal religious press are provided in George Marsden, *Fundamentalism and American Culture* (Oxford, UK: Oxford University Press, 1980), p. 175.

10. It is interesting to note that Bryan actually reflected an openness in his comments to interpreting the Bible's references to the six days of creation as geological ages; see Scopes Trial transcript, in Arthur Weinberg, ed., *Attorney for the Damned* (New York: Simon & Schuster, 1957), pp. 223–25.

11. The most devastating and influential critique of Fundamentalists during the trial was offered by H. L. Mencken, *Prejudices: Fifth Series* (New York, 1926).

12. Discussions of this dynamic in Fundamentalism after the Scopes Trial, including the "Great Reversal" of its political-ethical commitments are offered by Marsden, *Fundamentalism and American Culture*, pp. 85ff.; David Moberg, *The Great Reversal: Evangelism versus Social Concern* (Philadelphia: Lippincott, 1972).

13. For this analysis, see James Davison Hunter, *American Evangelicalism* (New Brunswick, NJ: Rutgers University Press, 1983), p. 39; Joel A. Carpenter, "From Fundamentalism to the New Evangelical Coalition," in *Evangelicalism and Modern America*, ed. George Marsden (Grand Rapids, MI: Eerdmans, 1984), pp. 6–7.

14. Growth in this era is noted by Marsden, *Fundamentalism and American Culture*, pp. 191–94; Carpenter, "From Fundamentalism," pp. 4, 6, 10–14.

15. Carl McIntire, "The Truth about the Federal Council of Churches and the Kingdom of God" (unpublished paper, Abilene Christian University Library, 1950); Billy James Hargis, *Communist America—Must It Be?* (1960) (Green Forest, AR: New Leaf Press, 1986); Bob Jones Sr., "Is Segregation Scriptural?" (radio address), April 17, 1960. Also see Robert B. Fowler, *A New Engagement: Evangelical Political Thought, 1966–1976* (Grand Rapids, MI: Eerdmans, 1982), pp. 13, 172; Erling Jorstad, *The Politics of Doomsday: Fundamentalists of the Far Right* (Nashville, TN: Abingdon, 1970).

16. These commitments were articulated by Harold Ockenga, "From Fundamentalism, through New Evangelicalism, to Evangelicalism," in *Evangelical Roots*, ed. Kenneth Kantzer (New York: Thomas Nelson, 1978), pp. 35–48; Edward John Carnell, *The Case for Orthodox Theology* (Philadelphia: Westminster Press, 1959), pp. 35–48; Carl F. H. Henry, *The Uneasy Conscience of Modern Fundamentalism* (Grand Rapids, MI: Eerdmans, 1947), especially p. 18.

17. A good example of this self-understanding is evident in Bernard Ramm, *The Evangelical Heritage* (Waco, TX: Word Publishers, 1973), pp. 50ff.

18. These convictions were articulated in early documents of the National Association of Evangelicals in its *United Evangelical Action*, August 15, 1945, p. 3; *United Evangelical Action*, November 1, 1945, p. 21; *United Evangelical Action*, September 1, 1945, p. 2.

19. Mark Noll, "Children of the Reformation in a Brave New World," *Dialog* 24 (1985): 176.

20. For a more detailed description of the issues at stake in the controversies over the Fuller theological faculty's views, see my *Evangelical Movement*, pp. 176–77.

21. Billy Graham, *London Observer*, April 24, 1955.

22. Billy Graham, *The Challenge* (Garden City, NY: Doubleday, 1969), p. 10; Billy Graham, *World Aflame* (Garden City, NY: Doubleday, 1965), pp. 176–76, 181, 187.

23. Carl F. H. Henry, *Aspects of Christian Social Ethics* (Grand Rapids, MI: Eerdmans, 1964), especially pp. 9, 16, 118, 127. For a more detailed discussion of Henry's contribution to developing Evangelical social consciousness and the reaction to it, see Fowler, *New Engagement*, pp. 77ff.

24. Carl F. H. Henry, *United Evangelical Action*, May 1, 1955, pp. 7ff.

25. Harold Lindsell, "Editorial," *Christianity Today*, November 10, 1972, 38–39; Harold Lindsell, "Editorial: Insecure Security," *Christianity Today*, July 28, 1972, pp. 23–24; Harold Lindsell, *The World, the Flesh, and the Devil* (Washington, DC: Canon Press, 1973), p. 47; cf. Carl F. H. Henry, "Editorial: Is Christian-Marxist Dialogue Possible?" *Christianity Today*, January 6, 1967, pp. 26–27.

26. For details on Bright's plan, see Jim Wallis, *God's Politics: Why the Right Gets It Wrong and the Left Doesn't Get It* (New York: HarperSanFrancisco, 2005), p. 358.

27. These statistics are available in Mark Noll, *American Evangelical Christianity: An Introduction* (Oxford, UK: Blackwell, 2001), pp. 22–23. For the Catholic and mainline church data, see Kevin Phillips, *American Theocracy: The Peril and Politics of Radical Religion, Oil, and Borrowed Money in the 21st Century* (New York: Viking, 2006), pp. 183–84; Susan Page, "Churchgoing Closely Tied to Voting Patterns," *USA Today*, June 2, 2004, at USATODAY.com.

Also see Sydney E. Ahlstrom, *A Religious History of the American People* (New Haven, CT: Yale University Press, 1972), pp. 921–22; chap. 8, nn. 1–3 for supporting evidence.

28. For passages from these traditions favoring welfare or a managed economy, see Augustine, *Epistles*, 153 (414), in *The Fathers of the Church*, vol. 20 (multivolume series; Washington, DC: Catholic University Press of America, 1947–1968), p. 302; *Catechism of the Catholic Church* (1994), 2425ff.; Martin Luther, *Ordinance of a Common Chest* (1523), in *Luther's Works*, vol. 45 (54 vols.; Philadelphia and St. Louis: Fortress and Concordia, 1955–1986), pp. 169–94; Martin Luther, *The Large Catechism* (1529), I.VII.249, in *The Book of Concord*, ed. Robert Kolb and Timothy J. Wengert (Minneapolis, MN: Fortress, 2000), p. 419; August Hermann Francke, "The Great Essay" (1704), in *A. H. Franckes Schrift über eine Reform des Erziehungs-und Bildungswesens als Ausgangspunkt eiener geistlichen und sozialen Neuordnung der Evangelischen Kirche des 18. Jahrhunderts: Der grosse Aufsatz*, ed. Otto Podczeck (Berlin: Sachsische Akademi der Wissenchaften, 1962); John Wesley, *Journal*, May 7, 1741; April 22, 1744, in *The Works of John Wesley*, Vol. 1 (repr. ed.; 14 vols.; Grand Rapids, MI: Baker Books, 1996), pp. 309, 458; The United Methodist Church, *Social Principles*, 163(E), in *The Book of Discipline of the United Methodist Church 2004*, pp. 116–17.

29. Robert Wuthnow, *The Restructuring of American Religion* (Princeton, NJ: Princeton University Press, 1990), p. 187; cf. Robert D. Putnam, *Bowling Alone: The Collapse and Revival of American Communality* (New York: Simon & Schuster, 2000), p. 161.

30. Robert Wuthnow, "The Political Rebirth of American Evangelicals," in *The New Christian Right*, ed. Robert C. Liebman and Robert Wuthnow (New York: Aldine, 1983), pp. 167–85.

31. For specific examples of these trends, see James Davison Hunter, *Evangelicalism: The Coming Generation* (Chicago: University of Chicago Press, 1987), especially pp. 121ff.; Marsden, *Fundamentalism and American Culture*, pp. 207ff.; Fowler, *A New Engagement*, pp. 192–93, 196–99.

32. "Half of U.S. Protestants Are 'Born Again' Christians," *The Gallup Poll* (September 26, 1976), pp. 1–7.

33. James L. Sullivan, quoted in "Born Again: The Year of the Evangelicals," *Newsweek*, October 25, 1976, p. 70. The first steps in the Fundamentalist takeover of the denomination and its war on the values of secularism date back to a 1969 sermon by the then denomination president W. A. Criswell, "Why I Preach that the Bible Is Literally True," reported in Mel White, *Religion Gone Bad: The Hidden Dangers of the Christian Right* (New York: Jeremy P. Tarcher/Penguin, 2006), pp. 39–40.

34. For a description of the evolution of this Republican strategy, see Phillips, *American Theocracy*, pp. x–xiii; Erling Jorstad, *The Politics of Moral-*

ism: The New Christian Right in American Life (Minneapolis, MN: Augsburg Publishing House, 1981), pp. 71–75. For documentation of the Right's origins in the controversy over Bob Jones University, see Randall Balmer, *Thy Kingdom Come: How the Religious Right Distorts the Faith and Threatens America* (New York: Basic, 2006), pp. 13–17; Ed Dobson, quoted in Michael Cromartie, ed., *No Longer Exiles: The Religious New Right in American Politics* (Washington, DC: Ethics and Public Policy Center, 1993), p. 52.

35. For these details, see "Taking Over the Republican Party," 2006, at www.theocracywatch.org.

36. For the complete report card of the Right's success in the 1980 national elections, see Jorstad, *Politics of Moralism*, pp. 100–104.

37. The publication in question with this impact, selling over 2 million copies, was Francis A. Schaeffer, *A Christian Manifesto* (Westchester, IL: Nims, 1981). For this assessment of the book's impact by an Evangelical insider, see White, *Religion Gone Bad*, pp. 33, 55–56. For Schaeffer's influence on Falwell, see the latter's *Strength for the Journey* (New York: Simon & Schuster, 1981), p. 361.

38. For these quotations and summaries I am indebted to Bill Press, *How the Republicans Stole Christmas: The Republican Party's Declared Monopoly on Religion and What Democrats Can Do to Take It Back* (New York: Doubleday, 2005), pp. 219–24. Especially see Joel Osteen, *Your Best Life Now* (New York: Warner, 2004), especially pp. 22, 43, where the mega-church pastor contends that "What you will receive is directly connected to how you believe"—that if we do our part God will do His part.

39. Cotton Mather, *Magnalia Christi Americana*, vol. 1 (1702; repr., Hartford, 1853), p. 61.

40. Oral Roberts, *Expect a Miracle: My Life and Ministry* (Nashville, TN: Thomas Nelson, 1995), especially p. 367; Bruce Wilkenson, *The Prayer of Jabez* (Sister, OR: Multnomah, 2000).

For the movement's roots, see Press, *How the Republicans Stole Christmas*, pp. 219–20; Phillips, *American Theocracy*, pp. 249–50.

CHAPTER 4

1. Jerry Falwell, "Future-Word," in Jerry Falwell, ed., *The Fundamentalist Phenomenon* (Garden City, NY: Doubleday, 1981), pp. 205–7, 210–11, 212–13.

2. Jerry Falwell, "Faith and Values Coalition: The 21st Century Moral Majority" November 10, 2004, at www.newsmax.com/archives/articles/2004; cf. www.answers.com/topic/faith-and-values-coalition.

3. For details on these organizations, see www.pfaw.org/pfaw/general/default. For more information on Dobson and much of the machinery of the Religious

Right, see Dan Gilgoff, *The Jesus Machine: How James Dobson and the Evangelical America Are Winning the Culture War* (New York: St. Martin's Press, 2007).

4. See Randall Balmer, *Thy Kingdom Come: How the Religious Right Distorts the Faith and Threatens America* (New York: Basic, 2006), pp. 199–200.

5. For this assessment of the clout of these groups, see Michael Lerner, *The Left Hand of God: Taking Back Our Country from the Religious Right* (New York: HarperSanFrancisco, 2006), p. 9. For a similar assessment, see www .theocracywatch.org. For the agenda of the Eagle Forum, see the address cited above in n. 3.

6. For the *ABC News* assessment, see Kevin Phillips, *American Theocracy: The Peril and Politics of Radical Religion, Oil, and Borrowed Money in the 21st Century* (New York: Viking, 2006), pp. 244–45; for the references in the *New York Times*, see www.nytimes.com/2004/08/28/politics/campaign/28conserve.html. Also see Mel White, *Religion Gone Bad: The Hidden Dangers of the Christian Right* (New York: Jeremy P. Tarcher/Penguin, 2006), pp. 241–45.

7. See Phillips, *American Theocracy*, pp. 244–45. To determine who among the members of the Council for National Policy are Reconstructionist in their orientation, compare en.wikipedia.org/wiki/Council_for_ National_Policy to en.wikipedia.org/wiki/Christian_Reconstructionism.

8. Pat Robertson, "The 700 Club" (television addresses), September 27, 1993; October 2, 1984; October 22, 1995; and n.d., in "Rhetoric of Intolerance: An Open Video to Pat Robertson," at www.soulforce.org/store. For Kennedy's quotation, see Bill Press, *How the Republicans Stole Christmas: The Republican Party's Declared Monopoly on Religion and What Democrats Can Do to Take It Back* (New York: Doubleday, 2005), pp. 38–39.

9. Pat Robertson, "The 700 Club" (television address), January 11, 1985.

10. Christian Coalition of America, "Principal Issues," at www.pfaw.org; for the Council for National Policy, see n. 6, above. On influencing the Republican Party, see the statement of the Christian Coalition of America's "Principal Issues," at www.pfaw.org, and statements by James Dobson's "Speech Before the Council for National Policy Meeting," February 7, 1998, reported in the *The Washington Times*, February 17, 1998 at www.wildershow.com/dobson.htm.

11. David Aikman, *A Man of Faith: The Spiritual Journey of George W. Bush* (Nashville, TN: W. Publishing Group, 2004).

12. For a good example of such a viewpoint, see "George Bush and God: A Hot Line to Heaven," *Economist*, December 16, 2004.

13. For this analysis I am indebted to Jim Wallis, *God's Politics: Why the Right Gets It Wrong and the Left Doesn't Get It* (New York: HarperSanFrancisco, 2005), pp. 143ff.

14. *The Westminster Confession of Faith* (1646), III, VII.

15. Richard Land reported that this is Bush's view of his call, as cited in Deborah Caldwell, "George Bush's Theology: Does President Believe He Has Divine Mandate?" *Religious News Service*, February 12, 2003. See also *The Westminster Confession*, VI, XX; D. L. Moody, *Secret Power; or, The Secret of Success in Christian Life and Christian Work* (Chicago, 1881).

16. *Westminster Confession*, V.

17. *Westminster Confession*, XXIII.

18. *Westminster Confession*, XXV.

19. Democrats need to take seriously this analysis, not merely resting content with more simplistic analyses of mainline Protestant and Catholic shifts to Republican support as have been offered by analysts like Kathleen Kennedy Townsend, *Failing America's Faithful* (New York: Warner Books, 2997), pp. 113–16, 128. If those committed to progressive social policies proceed as if the shift has been primarily the result of a backlash against the Civil Rights Movement, as she contends, and proceed accordingly, little will be done to challenge present voting trends of white members of these churches.

CHAPTER 5

1. For these observations about trends in our higher educational system, I am indebted to Allan Bloom, *The Closing of the American Mind: How Higher Education Has Failed Democracy and Impoverished the Souls of Today's Students* (New York: Simon & Schuster, 1987), pp. 131ff.

The application of these insights for theological education is based on my own observations.

2. For these insights and many of the points I will make, I have been inspired by the provocative analysis of Robert Benne, *The Paradoxical Vision: A Public Theology for the Twenty-first Century* (Minneapolis, MN: Fortress, 1995), pp. 26ff. For the bohemian character of the higher educational establishment, see Christopher Lasch, *The Revolt of the Elites and the Betrayal of Democracy* (New York: Norton, 1995), pp. 233–34.

3. For more detailed exposition and documentation of Common Sense Realism on these Founders, see my *A Common Sense Theology: The Bible, Faith, and American Society* (Macon, GA: Mercer University Press, 1995), pp. 101ff.

4. Thomas Reid, *Essays on the Intellectual Powers of Man* (1785), ed. A. D. Woozley (London, 1941), pp. 258, 263, 309, 364, 403, 437–38.

5. John Locke, *Essay Concerning Human Understanding* (1690), II.ii.2; IV.iv; IV.x.

6. Peter Williams Jr., "Oration on the Abolition of the Slave Trade" (1808), in *Negro Orators and Their Orations*, ed. Carter G. Woodson (Washington, DC,

1925), pp. 33–41; William Yates, *Rights of Colored Men to Suffrage, Citizenship, and Trial by Jury* (Philadelphia: Merrihaw and Gunn, 1838), p. 34.

7. Immanuel Kant, *Critique of Pure Reason*, trans. Norman Kemp Smith (New York: St. Martin's, 1965), pp. 41–62, 87–89, 277–75.

8. George Barna, *What Americans Believe* (Ventura, CA: Regal, 1991), pp. 83–85.

9. A theologian no less famous than Karl Barth made this claim in his *Protestant Thought: From Rousseau to Ritschl*, trans. Brian Cozens (New York: Simon & Schuster, 1959), pp. 306–7. Also see B. A. Gerrish, *A Prince of the Church: Schleiermacher and the Beginnings of Modern Theology* (Philadelphia: Fortress, 1984), pp. 1ff.

10. Friedrich Schleiermacher, *The Christian Faith*, vol. I, ed. H. R. Mackintosh and J. S. Stewart (New York: Harper & Row, 1963), pp. 12–18, 76–83.

11. For such an assessment of the connections between Schleiermacher and Kant, see Barth, *Protestant Thought*, especially p. 344.

12. Two important Catholic theologians who embody these Kantian suppositions are Bernard Lonergan (his Transcendental Method), *Theological Investigations*, vol. IX (New York: Seabury, 1972), pp. 28–33, and one of his famous American admirers, David Tracy (his Method of Critical Correlation), *Blessed Rage for Order* (New York: Seabury, 1978), pp. 43–56, 74–75, 84, 134. Among famous Protestant proponents of the Method of Correlation (or something like it) and its Kantian suppositions include Paul Tillich, *Systematic Theology*, vol. 1 (3 vols. in one; Chicago: University of Chicago Press, 1967), pp. 3–8, 59, 66; Paul Ricoeur, *Essays in Biblical Interpretation*, ed. Lewis Mudge (Philadelphia: Fortress, 1980), pp. 108, 143.

13. Tony Campolo, *Speaking My Mind* (Nashville, TN: W. Publishing, 2004), pp. 3ff.

14. For documentation of the mainline Protestant denominations' affirmation of these issues and Catholicism's preoccupation with justice and civil rights issues, see my *The Cutting Edge: How Churches Speak on Social Issues* (Geneva: WCC Publications, 1993); as well as my "Homosexuality and the Churches: A Quest for the Nicene Vision," *Journal of Ecumenical Studies* 30, no. 5–4 (Summer–Fall, 1993): 354–71.

15. Max Weber, *The Protestant Ethic and the Spirit of Capitalism*, trans. Talcott Parsons (London: Allen & Unwin, 1930). For these insights about the way in which Americans have received his thought, see Bloom, *The Closing of the American Mind*, pp. 150–51, 337–38.

16. Friedrich Nietzsche, "Thus Spoke Zarathustra" (1892), I.Pro.3,4; I.22.3, in *The Portable Nietzsche*, ed. Walter Kaufmann (New York: Viking, 1968), pp. 124–26; 190–91; Friedrich Nietzsche, "On Ethics" (1868), in *Portable Nietzsche*, pp. 30–31; Friedrich Nietzsche, "Toward a Genealogy of Morals" (1887), p. 10, in *Portable Nietzsche*, p. 451; Friedrich Nietzsche, "Revaluation of All Values"

(1888), Preface, in *Portable Nietzsche*, 568–69. For these observations about the impact of Nietzsche on the American academy and on society as a whole, I am again indebted to Bloom, *Closing of the American Mind*, pp. 146–54. For examples of the relativism in reading texts, see the references above in n. 12.

17. For evidences of Freud's cynical realism about human nature, see his *Civilization and Its Discontents*, trans. James Strachey (New York: Norton, 1961), pp. 30, 89–90. For a similar assessment that Carl Jung's optimistic adaptation of Freud has had greater impact on modern psychology than Freud's own realism, see Calvin Hall and Gardner Lindzey, *Theories of Personality*, 2nd ed. (New York: Wiley, 1970), pp. 111–12.

18. Regarding our therapeutic culture, the insights of Christopher Lasch, in *The Culture of Narcissism: American Life in an Age of Diminishing Expectations* (New York: Norton, 1979), pp. 33ff., remain relevant over twenty-five years after he made these points. Also see his *Revolt of the Elites*, pp. 219, 221.

The Prosperity Gospel described in the preceding chapter offers a good example of how this thinking has permeated the Church, even in Evangelical circles. The popularity in theological education of a book widely used as early as the 1950s by Ruel Howe, *Man's Need and God's Action* (New York: Seabury, 1953), illustrates the impact of this way of thinking on the academy.

19. Lasch, *Revolt of the Elites*, pp. 180, 207. The highly influential critique of the doctrine of Original Sin was first mounted at a meeting of psychologists by Krister Stendahl, *Paul among Jews and Gentiles, and Other Essays* (Philadelphia: Fortress, 1976), pp. 78–96.

20. Some hints of this thinking are evident in Tillich, *Systematic Theology*, vol. 2, p. 248. Also see David E. Roberts, *Psychotherapy and a Christian View of Man* (New York: Scribner, 1950), pp. 129–38.

21. For the premiere spokesperson for DeConstruction and for indications of how he has been interpreted in America, see Jacques Derrida, *Limited Inc.* (Evanston, IL: Northwestern University Press, 1977), pp. 105–6, 131, 145. Also see Edward Said, *Orientalism* (New York: Vintage, 1994), especially p. 10, who claims that standards are never disinterested acts of judgment, but always assertions of power grounded in ideology and self-interest.

CHAPTER 6

1. Barna Research Group, "Christians Say They Do Best at Relationships, Worst in Bible Knowledge," *The Barna Update*, June 14, 2005, at www.barna .org. Also see "Editor in Chief's Pulse of the Nation," *The Gallup Poll*, December 17, 2002, at poll.gallup.com/nationspulse.

2. Richard Quebedeaux, *By What Authority: The Rise of Personality Cults in American Christianity* (San Francisco: Harper & Row, 1982), pp. 151–52.

3. Alan Wolfe, *Moral Freedom: The Search for Virtue in a World of Choice* (New York: Norton, 2001), p. 185; Quebedeaux, *By What Authority*, pp. 13–131; David S. Schuller, Merton P. Strommen, and Milo L. Brekke, eds., *Ministry in America* (San Francisco: Harper & Row, 1980), pp. 29ff.

4. Quebedeaux, *By What Authority*, pp. 147, 151–52. For the analysis of the dominance of the "Team Management" concept of modern business administration and its implications, see Richard Sennett, *The Corrosion of Character: The Personal Consequences of Work in the New Capitalism* (New York: Norton, 1998), pp. 24, 106ff.

5. Quebedeaux, *By What Authority*, p. 152. See Christopher Lasch, *The Revolt of the Elites and the Betrayal of Democracy* (New York: Norton, 1995), pp. 205–6, for a description of contemporary American religion as a culture in which Sin is abolished in favor of a humanistic acceptance of self and body. Also see Barna Research Group, "Beliefs: Salvation," 2005, at www.barna.org; "Beliefs: The Bible," 2005, at www.barna.org.

For the National Election Pool exit poll data on the 2006 elections, see Pew Research Center Observation Deck, "Election '06: Big Changes in Some Key Groups," November 16, 2006, at pewresearch.org/obdeck=93.

6. Joseph Cardinal Ratzinger, "Pre-Conclave and Papal Election Mass Homily," April 18, 2005, at www.freepublic.com/focus/f-religion/1385934/posts. Also see Joseph Cardinal Ratzinger, *Salt of the Earth* (San Francisco: Ignatius, 1997), p. 134.

7. Barna Research Group, "Americans Are Most Likely to Base Truth on Feelings," *The Barna Update*, February 12, 2002, at www.barna.org; George Barna, *What Americans Believe* (Ventura, CA: Regal, 1991), pp. 83–85.

8. G. Lloyd Rediger and Kevin Leicht have noted that the firing rate for ministers is higher than that of the national labor force, even higher than the rate of dismissal among NFL football coaches. A Winter 1996 report of a study by *Leadership* magazine indicated that nearly one-fourth of all clergy from various denominations have been fired at least once. Data cited in "Turnover in the Clergy: Why Don't Clergy Keep Their Jobs?" (2006) at atheism.about.com. Also see Jackson W. Carroll, "Protestant Pastoral Ministry at the Beginning of the New Millennium" (paper presented at the Society for the Scientific Study of Religion and Religious Research Association, Houston, TX, October 18, 2001), p. 1. See also Larry Witham, *Who Shall Lead Them? The Future of Ministry in America* (London: Oxford University Press, 2005), p. 90, has reported that over 760 Southern Baptist Convention pastors were fired in 2000, a figure that was merely part of a fifteen-year pattern in the convention.

9. For documentation of these points with regard to mainline Protestant denominational bodies, see chap. 5, n. 14. Not just at the denominational level have the mainline churches embraced the new morality. Barna Research Group

reported in "Practical Outcomes Replace Biblical Principles as the Moral Standard," September 10, 2001, p. 5, that 54 percent of mainline Protestants believed in the acceptability of "shacking up." A year later, only 49 percent of Protestant teens deemed premarital sex wrong (reported in *The Gallup Poll Tuesday Briefing*, April 2002, p. 38). The new morality's appropriation by Catholics was reported in *The Gallup Poll Tuesday Briefing,* April 2005, pp. 92–93: 37 percent deemed abortion morally acceptable, 48 percent regarded homosexuality as acceptable, and 68 percent considered abortion morally appropriate. The reception of relativism in the American pews was evidenced as early as December 1999 (see page 53 of the same source). The Gallup poll reported that only 16 percent of religious Americans regarded their own religion as the best path, while 82 percent regard religions other than their own equally good as those they espouse.

10. Reported in "Twelve Tribes: Which Issues Mattered in 2004?" at www.beliefnet.com/story; "The Twelve Tribes of American Politics," p. 4, at www.beliefnet.com.story.153.

11. See John C. Green, Corwin E. Smidt, et al., "The American Religious Landscape and the 2004 Presidential Vote: Increased Polarization," p. 9, at pewforum.org.publications.

12. Reported in "The Twelve Tribes of American Politics," on www.beliefnet.com.story. 153.

13. Barna Research Group, "Beliefs: The Bible," 2005, at www.barna.org/FlexPage.aspx. A more recent Gallup poll reported May 22, 2006, as reported at www.pollingreport.com/religion.htm, finds that only three in ten Americans claim that Bible is literally the Word of God. But this somewhat conflicts with a November 19, 2004, poll that found that almost one in two Americans took a literalistic position on Creation. But the May 2006 Gallup poll is not necessarily that much in conflict with the other polls, since it still found that nearly seven in ten Americans would have the Bible be read literally at least on many occasions. See www.pollingreport.com/religion.htm.

CHAPTER 7

1. On the political shifts of the Asian-American community, see Franklin Foer, "Asian America Discovers Identity Politics: Reorientation," *The New Republic* (July 2001): 15–17. On the shifts in the black community, see Hanes Walton and Robert Charles Smith, *American Politics and the African American Quest for Universal Freedom* (New York: Longman, 2003), especially pp. 135ff. Also see "Veterans of the Civil Rights Movement—Timeline," p. 10, at www.crmvet.org/tim/timhis60.htm. On union involvement (which assumes Democratic loyalty) of the Orthodox, especially the Russians, see Paul R.

Magocsi, "Russian Americans," p. 9, at www.everyculture.com. For an analysis of historic trends in Asian-American politics, see Gorden H. Chang, *Asian Americans and Politics: Perspectives, Experiences, Prospects* (Washington, DC: Woodrow Wilson Center Press, 2001). For the pro–labor union (and Democratic) orientation of Catholics, see Sydney E. Ahlstrom, *A Religious History of the American People* (4th print.; New Haven, CT: Yale University Press, 1974), pp. 1003, 1007–11. Kathleen Kennedy Townsend [*Failing America's Faithful: How Today's Churches Are Mixing God with Politics and Losing Their Way Back* (New York: Warner Books, 2007), pp. 65–87] echoes the long history of American Catholicism's commitment to social justice and the welfare of the labor force. These points about the historical Catholic identification with the Democratic Party are totally neglected in the analysis of the new Republican orientation by Ray Suarez, *The Holy Vote: The Politics of Faith in* America (New York: Harper Collins, 2006), pp. 185–216. This seriously undermines the helpfulness of his analysis. For American Lutheranism's alignment with the unions, especially after World War I, see E. Clifford Nelson, ed., *The Lutherans in North America* (Philadelphia: Fortress, 1975), pp. 275, 386. Also see Paul Kieppner, *The Cross of Culture* (New York: Free Press, 1970).

2. Fourth National Survey of Religion and Politics, November-December 2004, reported in "2004 Election Exit Poll Results," at www.beliefnet.com/story/155/story; Fourth National Survey of Religion and Politics, November-December 2004, reported in John C. Green, Corwin E. Smidt, et al., "The American Religious Landscape and the 2004 Presidential Vote: Increased Polarization," p. 4, at pewforum.org.publications.

Exit poll data from the National Election Pool 2006 in Scott Keeter, "Election '06: Big Changes in Some Key Groups," Pew Research Center, at pewresearch.org/obdeckID=93. Also see Pew Research Center Observation Deck, "Centrists Deliver for Democrats," at pewresearch.org/obdeckID=88.

3. Tom Heinen, "Presidential Race Finds Home in Churches," *Milwaukee Journal Sentinel*, September 19, 2004; Albert Menendez, "Bush Wins Again with Big Assist from Religious Conservatives," in *Voice of Reason*, 2004, no. 4. For another analysis highlighting the German identification with Republicans and the continuing Scandinavian (especially Norwegian) identification with the Democratic Party, see Kevin Phillips, *American Theocracy: The Peril and Politics of Radical Religion, Oil, and Borrowed Money in the 21st Century* (New York: Viking, 2006), pp. 390–92.

4. See Mark Ellingsen, *Blessed Are the Cynical: How Original Sin Can Make America a Better Place* (Grand Rapids, MI: Brazos, 2003), especially pp. 159–79.

5. For these statistics, see Robert Wuthnow, *The Restructuring of American Religion* (Princeton, NJ: Princeton University Press, 1988), pp. 85–86.

6. Lutherans and Catholics in Dialogue VII, *Justification by Faith* (Common Statement) (1983); cf. Lutheran World Federation–Catholic Church, *Joint Declaration on the Doctrine of Justification* (1997).

7. For a historical overview of these developments, see Nelson, *Lutherans in North America*.

8. Reported in Barna Research Online, "Religious Beliefs Vary Widely by Denominations," 2001, at www.barna.org.

9. Reported in www.beliefnet.com/story/155; John C. Green, Corwin E. Smidt, et al., "The American Religious Landscape and the 2004 Presidential Vote: Increased Polarization," p. 4, at pewforum.org.publications.

10. Poll results in *The Gallup Poll Tuesday Briefing*, April 2005, pp. 92–93; *Gallup Poll Monthly*, June 1992, pp. 4–5. Cf. John McGreevy, "Shifting Allegiances: Catholics, Democrats and the GOP," *Commonweal* 133, no. 16 (September 22, 2006).

CHAPTER 8

1. Fourth National Survey of Religion and Politics, November-December 2004, reported in John C. Green, Corwin E. Smidt, et al., "The American Religious Landscape and the 2004 Presidential Vote: Increased Polarization," pp. 2, 4, 9, at pewforum.org.publications; Asian American Legal Defense and Education Fund, "APIA Vote Exit Polling Results," November 10, 2004, 2, at www.apiavote.org/2004ExitPollResults; Zogby International Poll, reported in Jim Lobe, "U.S. Election: Minorities Backed Kerry," *Inter Press Service News Agency*, November 5, 2004, p. 2, at www.ipsnews.net/intrerna.asp. For the 2006 exit poll results conducted by the National Election Pool, see Scott Keeter, "Election '06: Big Changes in Some Key Groups," Pew Research Center, at pewresearch.org/obdeckID=93.

2. Hartford Institute for Religion Research, *Faith Communities Today* (March 2001): 16, 46. For an earlier survey with similar results, see C. Eric Lincoln and Lawrence H. Mamiya, *The Black Church in the African American Experience* (Durham, NC: Duke University Press, 1990), pp. 168–69, 240ff.

3. Reported in Kevin Phillips, *American Theocracy: The Peril and Politics of Radical Religion, Oil, and Borrowed Money in the 21st Century* (New York: Viking, 2006), p. 195.

4. James D. Bratt, *Dutch Calvinism in Modern America* (Grand Rapids, MI: Eerdmans, 1984), especially pp. 74–76, 155.

5. Cornel West, *Race Matters* (2nd ed.; New York: Vintage, 2001), pp. 95, 97, 158; Anthony B. Pinn, *Terror and Triumph: The Nature of Black Religion* (Minneapolis, MN: Fortress, 2003), pp. 144–45, 175.

6. Tamar Jacoby, "Commentary," *Asian America* (July-August 2000); Steve Sailer, "Asian Americans Are Moving to the Left," for UPI (November 12, 2000), at www.isteve.com/2000. The results of recent elections will force conservative Evangelical commentators like Tony Campolo, *Speaking My Mind* (Nashville, TN: W. Publishing, 2004), especially p. 24, to rethink their claims about the Republican loyalties of Asian-Americans.

7. "Americans On—Church Attendance," *Hear the Issues*, April 2006, at www.heartheissues.co/americanson-churchattendance042006, based on a 2006 Gallup poll.

8. Barna Research Group, "The Bible," at www.barna.org/FlexPage.aspx; John Green and Steven Waldman, "The Twelve Tribes of American Politics," (2005), *Beliefnet*, at www.beliefnet.com.xtory/153.

9. Fourth National Survey of Religion and Politics, in Green and Waldman.

CHAPTER 9

1. For an elaboration of their conservative theological convictions, see my *Reclaiming Our Roots: From Martin Luther to Martin Luther King Jr.,* vol. 2 (Harrisburg, PA: Trinity, 1999), especially pp. 325–27, 362–64.

2. Jim Wallis, *God's Politics: Why the Right Gets It Wrong and the Left Doesn't Get It* (New York: HarperSanFrancisco, 2005), especially pp. vi–vii; Randall Balmer, *Thy Kingdom Come: How the Religious Right Distorts the Faith and Threatens America* (New York: Basic, 2006), pp. 190–91; Bob Edgar, *Middle Church: Reclaiming the Moral Values of the Faithful Majority from the Religious Right* (New York: Simon & Schuster, 2006), pp. 95ff.; Michael Lerner, *The Left Hand of God: Taking Back Our Country from the Religious Right* (New York: HarperSanFrancisco, 2006), pp. 110, 365. To Edgar's credit he does recognize that non-Christians can embody the values of his Christian politics (pp. 204–8).

3. Bill Press, *How the Republicans Stole Christmas: The Republican Party's Declared Monopoly on Religion and What Democrats Can Do to Take It Back* (New York: Doubleday, 2005), pp. 60–66, 240ff.; Jimmy Carter, *Our Endangered Values: America's Moral Crisis* (New York: Simon & Schuster, 2005), pp. 18, 57–64; Barack Obama, *The Audacity of Hope: Thoughts on Reclaiming the American Dream* (New York: Crown, 2006), especially pp. 86, 214–15. Also see Gregory A. Boyd, *The Myth of a Christian Nation: How the Quest for Political Power Is Destroying the Church* (Grand Rapids, MI: Zondervan, 2005), especially pp. 14–15, 35–44, 127–41. To his credit, he even refers to the doctrine of Sin in guiding his political proposals.

4. Alexander Hamilton made this point in "No. 78," in *The Federalist Papers* (New York: Penguin, 1961), p. 468; see also "Law," in *World Book Ency-*

clopedia, vol. 11 (1961), pp. 117–18, which claims all jurisprudence reflects in some form the Ten Commandments. The Declaration of Independence refers to "Laws of Nature." See also Thomas Jefferson, "Letter to Dr. Thomas Cooper" (1814), in *Writings* (New York: Library of America, 1984), pp. 1324–27.

5. For background on this new marketing style and its successes, see Douglas B. Sosnik, Matthew J. Dowd, and Ron Fournier, *Applebee's America: How Successful Political, Business, and Religious Leaders Connect with the New American Community* (New York: Simon & Schuster, 2006).

6. Stephen Carter, *The Culture of Disbelief: How American Law and Politics Trivialize Devotion* (New York: Basic, 1993), pp. 23, 25.

7. Press, *How the Republicans*, pp. 60ff. Ray Suarez, *The Holy Vote: The Politics of Faith in America* (New York: HarperCollins, 2006), pp. 113–14. Among the first post-Medieval scholars to champion this way of thinking include Hugo Grotius, *De Jure Belli et Pacis*, vol. 2, trans. Francis W. Kelsey (Oxford, UK: Oxford University Press, 1925), especially pp. 11, 13. For others who championed the divorce of the concept from theology, see Francis Oakley, *Natural Law, Laws of Nature, Natural Rights* (New York: Continuum, 2005), especially pp. 21, 63ff.

8. Plato, *The Republic*, II.XIII.435; II.XIV.441; IV.XXXIV.591; Aristotle, *Nichomachean Ethics*, V.VII.

9. Cicero, *Laws*, II.IV.8–11; Marcus Aurelius, *Meditations*, IV.4.

10. Justin Martyr, *Dialogue with Trypho*, 45.4; Tertullian, *Against Marcion*, 5.15.3.

11. Origen, *Against Celsus*, 5.37; Augustine, *On the Spirit and the Letter* (412), XXI.36; Augustine, *On Free Will*, vi.14–15; Augustine, *City of God* (413–426), II.4; V.12.

12. Peter Abelard, *Dialogue between a Philosopher, a Jew, and a Christian*; Thomas Aquinas, *Summa Theologica*, I/II, Q. XCI, Arts.I–IV. For the scholastic indebtedness to Plato's *Timaeus*, see Oakley, *Natural Law*, 32.

13. For these insights I am indebted to Forest McDonald, *Novus Ordo Seculorum: The Intellectual Origins of the Constitution* (Lawrence: University of Kansas Press, 1985), p. 58.

14. John Locke, *Second Treatise on Civil Government* (1690), pp. 124ff.; cf. the critics cited above in n. 7.

15. Thomas Reid, *Practical Ethics* (Princeton, NJ: Princeton University Press, 1990), pp. 254ff.; Thomas Reid, *Essays on the Active Powers of Man*, in *The Works of Thomas Reid*, vol. 2 (Edinburgh: Maclachlon and Stewart, 1872), pp. 590, 647, 652.

16. Edward O. Wilson, *Sociobiology: The New Synthesis* (Cambridge, MA: Harvard University Press, 1974), especially p. 4; cf. Mary Midgley, *Beast and Man: The Roots of Human Nature* (Ithaca, NY: Cornell University Press, 1978), pp. 138, 198–99.

17. James Madison, "No. 51," in *Federalist Papers*, p. 324.

18. Alexander Hamilton, "No. 29," in *Federalist Papers*, p. 186; Alexander Hamilton, "No. 31," in *Federalist Papers*, p. 193; Alexander Hamilton, "No. 75," in *Federalist Papers*, p. 448; Alexander Hamilton, "No. 84," in *Federalist Papers*, p. 517; Alexander Hamilton, "No. 85," in *Federalist Papers*, p. 523.

19. James Madison, "No. 43," in *Federalist Papers*, p. 279; Hamilton, "No. 78," p. 468.

20. Thomas Jefferson, "Letter to Messrs. Nehemiah Dodge and Others, a Committee of the Danbury Baptist Association in the State of Connecticut" (1802), in *Writings* (New York: Library of America, 1984), p. 510.

21. John Calvin, *Institutio Christianae Religionis* (1559), II.VIII.102.

22. John Witherspoon, Lectures I and II, *An Annotated Edition of Lectures on Moral Philosophy*, ed. Jack Scott (Newark: University of Delaware Press, 1982), pp. 64–66, 78–81; cf. L. Gordon Tait, *The Piety of John Witherspoon* (Louisville, KY: Geneva Press, 2001), p. 124.

23. Results reported in "Public Divided on Origins of Life: Religion a Strength and Weakness for Both Parties," in *The Pew Forum on Religion and Public Life*, August 30, 2005, at pewforum.org. This majority is reflected insofar as 39 percent of the public feel there is too little discussion of faith and prayer by political leaders and another 27 percent feel we have just the right amount.

24. See Oakley, *Natural Law*.

25. Locke, *Second Treatise*, pp. 5, 6.

26. Reid, *Essays*, p. 647.

27. Benjamin Franklin, "Letter to Madame Briloon" (1778), in *Writings* (New York: Library of America, 1987), p. 920.

28. Press, *How the Republicans*, pp. 60ff.

29. Martin Luther, *The Small Catechism* (1529), I.5., in *The Book of Concord*, eds. Robert Kolb and Timothy J. Wengert (Minneapolis, MN: Fortress, 2000), p. 352.

30. Assembly of Divines at Westminster, *The Larger Catechism* (1647), Q. 135.

31. Luther, *Small Catechism*, I.7, 353.

32. Martin Luther, *The Large Catechism* (1529), I.7.

33. Assembly of Divines, *Larger Catechism*, Q. 141; John Wesley, *Explanatory Notes upon the Old Testament* (1755–1756), Exodus 20:15; Catholic Church, *Catechism of the Catholic Church* (1994), pp. 2446, 2448.

34. For details and documentation about pre-Augustinian formulations of the doctrine of Original Sin, as well as concerning the context in which the African Father developed the doctrine, see my *Blessed Are the Cynical: How Original Sin Can Make America a Better Place* (Grand Rapids, MI: Brazos, 2003), pp. 34ff.

35. Augustine, *On the Spirit*, p. 5.

36. Augustine, *Confessions* (399), VI.XII.22; VI.XV.25; XII.VII.8; Augustine, *City of God*, XI7V.15.

37. Augustine, *On Marriage and Concupiscence* (419/420), LXXI.24–LXXII.25; cf. Augustine, *To Simplician—On Various Questions* (395/396), II.20.

38. Augustine, *Confessions*, II.VI.12–13.

39. Augustine, *Ten Homilies on the Epistle of John to the Parthians* (ca. 417), 8.9.

40. Anthony Walsh, *The Science of Love: Understanding Love and Its Effects on Mind and Body* (Buffalo, NY: Prometheus, 1991).

41. James Madison, *Notes of Debates in the Federal Convention of 1787, Reported by James Madison* (New York: Library of America, 1987), pp. 34, 52, 131, 233–34, 311–12, 322–23.

42. Benjamin Franklin, "The Busy-Body, No. 4," in *Writings*, p. 98.

43. James Madison, "No. 10" and "No. 51," *The Federalist Papers*, pp. 77–84, 324–25.

44. Madison, *Notes of Debates*, p. 4. Compare with Karl Marx, "Contribution to the Critique of Hegel's Philosophy of Right. Introduction" (1844), in Early Writings, trans. and ed. B. Bottomore (New York: McGraw-Hill, 1963), pp. 55–59.

45. James Madison, "No. 49," *The Federalist Papers*, pp. 314–15.

46. Madison, "No. 51," p. 323.

47. James Madison, "No. 63," *The Federalist Papers*, p. 384.

48. John Witherspoon, *Speech in Congress upon the Confederation*, in *Works*, vol. 9 (9 vols.; Edinburgh: Ogle & Aikman, 1805), p. 139.

49. Alexander Hamilton, "No. 15," *Federalist Papers*, p. 110.

50. Madison, "No. 51," 325; cf. Madison, "No. 10," pp. 78, 79.

51. Witherspoon, *An Annotated Edition of Lectures*, p. 144.

52. Alexander Hamilton, "Report on Manufactures," *Papers*, vol. 10, ed. Harold Syrett (26 vols.; New York, 1961–1979), pp. 266–67.

Especially relevant would be a study of Hamilton's economics, his concern to protect American businesses by means of high import taxes, and his advocacy of a tax policy that raised funds primarily from commerce, not from landowners and laborers. Such a study is beyond the scope of this work, deserving another book sometime.

53. Thomas Frank, *What's the Matter with Kansas? How Conservatives Won the Heart of America* (New York: Henry Holt, 2004).

54. Locke, *Second Treatise*, p. 31.

55. Thomas Jefferson, *Notes on the State of Virginia* (1787), p. XIV.

56. Thomas Jefferson, "Letter to James Madison" (1785), in *Writings*, pp. 841–42.

57. Benjamin Franklin, "Letter to Robert Morris" (1783), in *Writings*, pp. 1081–82.

58. Alexander Hamilton, "No. 36," in *Federalist Papers*, pp. 222–23.

59. James Madison, "Parties" (1792), in *The Papers of James Madison, 1791–1793*, vol. 14 (Charlottesville: University Press of Virginia, 1983), p. 197.

60. See Bernard Bailyn, *Apologia of Robert Keayne: the Last Will and Testimony of One, Robert Keayne* (New York: Harper & Row, 1965).

61. *The Westminster Confession of Faith* (1646), VI. I have deliberately described the version of Augustine's view of Sin, which was appropriated by the Protestant Reformers and their Puritan heirs.

For the alternative, or characteristically Roman Catholic, interpretation of the African Father's view of Sin, see my *The Richness of Augustine: His Contextual and Pastoral Theology* (Louisville, KY: Westminster John Knox Press, 2005), especially pp. 73–82.

CHAPTER 10

1. See Karl Barth, *Church Dogmatics*, vol. I/1, trans. G. T. Thomson (Edinburgh: T & T Clark, 1936), pp. 373 ff.; Karl Barth, *Church Dogmatics*, vol. I/2, ed. G. W. Bromiley and T. F. Torrance (Edinburgh: T & T Clark, 1956), pp. 722–40.

2. Karl Barth was author of the anti-Hitler document of the confessing Church, *The Barmen Declaration* (1934). For his Socialist predispositions, see *Church Dogmatics*, vol. III/4, ed. G. W. Bomley and T. F. Torance (Edinburgh: T. & T. Clark, 1961), pp. 543 ff.

3. For these commitments, see Hans Frei, *The Eclipse of Biblical Narrative* (New Haven, CT: Yale University Press, 1974), pp. viii, 4 ff. Also see Mark Ellingsen, my *The Integrity of Biblical Narrative* (Minneapolis, MN: Augsburg Fortress, 1990).

4. Joseph Cardinal Ratzinger, *"In the Beginning . . .": A Catholic Understanding of Creation and the Fall*, trans. Boniface Ramsey (Grand Rapids, MI: Eerdmans, 1990), pp. 4–5. Also see Mark Ellingsen, my "How Conservative is Benedict XVI?" *Theology Today* (October 2005), pp. 390–91.

5. For this assessment of the African-American Church's characteristic view of the Bible, see Milton G. Sernett, "Black Religion and the Question of Evangelical Identity," in *The Variety of American Evangelicalism*, ed. Donald W. Dayton and Robert K. Johnston (Downers Grove, IL: InterVarsity Press, 1991), especially p. 143. Poll results confirming the general Biblical literalism of the Black Church can be identified in the Fourth National Survey of Religion and

Politics (2004), reported in John Green and Steven Waldman, "The Twelve Tribes of American Politics," p. 7, at www.beliefnet.com/story/153.

CONCLUSION

1. Jim Wallis, *God's Politics: Why the Right Gets It Wrong and the Left Doesn't Get It* (New York: HaperSanFrancisco, 2005), especially pp. 374, 387; Michael Lerner, *The Left Hand of God: Taking Back Our Country from the Religious Right* (New York: Harper SanFrancisco, 2006), pp. 363ff.

2. See chap. 9, n. 7, for references.

3. Catholic Church, *Catechism if the Catholic Church* (1992), pp. 2207–13, 2228, 2426–49, 2487, 2536–37; Synod of Heidelberg, *The Heidelberg Catechism* (1563), Q. 110; Assembly of Divines at Westminster, *The Larger Catechism* (1647), Qq. 130, 139, 141, 145, 147; Martin Luther, *The Large Catechism* (1529), I.4, 7–10; Martin Luther, *The Small Catechism* (1529), I.5–9.

4. The data are evident in that, according to the U.S. Census Bureau, *Statistical Abstract of the United States, 2004–2006*, table 113, of the ten states with the highest rates of divorce, six of them are among the poorest. See U.S. Census Bureau News, August 30, 2005, at www.census.gov/Press-Release/www.realeas/archives/income_wealth/005647.

5. Thomas Frank, *What's the Matter with Kansas? How Conservatives Won the Heart of America* (New York: Henry Holt, 2005), pp. 242ff.

6. For these statistics, see these denominations' 2004–2006 membership reports, available in Eileen W. Linder, ed., *Yearbook of American and Canadian Churches, 2006* (Nashville, TN: Abingdon, 2006). On the historic Republican dispositions of a number of the mainline Protestant denominations, see Lyman A. Kellstedt, John C. Green, James L. Guth, and Corwin E. Smidt, "It's the Culture Stupid! 1992 and Our Political Future," *First Things* 42 (April 1994): 28–33; Sydney Ahlstrom, *A Religious History of the American People* (New Haven, CT: Yale University Press, 1972), especially pp. 924–25. But Ahlstrom, p. 921, also points out those Northern-based denominations that supported the New Deal in the 1930s. For the insight that not all mega-church members and Southern Baptists vote Republican, see Douglas B. Sosnik, Matthew J. Dowd, and Ron Fournier, *Applebee's American: How Successful Political, Business, and Religious Leaders Connect with the New American Community* (New York: Simon & Schuster, 2006), especially pp. 7, 121.

The liberal, pro-Democratic bent of the mainline Protestant denominations is evident in their official church social statements issued from 1960 though the 1980s. For a detailed analysis, see my *The Cutting Edge: How Churches Speak On Social Issues* (Geneva: WCC Publications, 1993), especially pp. 163–79,

195–96, 198, 199, 201, 203–9, 214, 216–17, 307–10, 312–15, 318–26, 328–32, 335–39, 341–42. At least as recently as the mid-1970s, member surveys of American churches indicated an overall positive, at least mixed assessment of taking an active role in working for minorities and oppressed people; see David S. Schuller, Merton P. Strommen, and Milo L. Brekke, eds., *Ministry in America* (San Francisco: Harper & Row, 1980), pp. 42–45.

Index